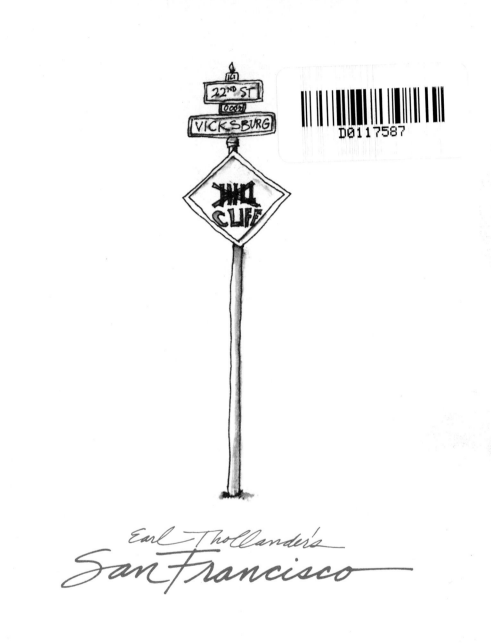

Earl Thollander's
*San Francisco*

*Mural at Langton and Howard Street Mini Park*

# Earl Thollander's
# San Francisco

## 30 WALKING TOURS
## FROM THE EMBARCADERO
## TO THE
## GOLDEN GATE

*Clarkson N. Potter, Inc. / Publishers*
DISTRIBUTED BY CROWN PUBLISHERS, INC. NEW YORK

*To Nor and Charles*

*Books by Earl Thollander*

Back Roads of California
Back Roads of Oregon
Back Roads of Washington
Back Roads of New England
Back Roads of the Carolinas
Back Roads of Arizona
Back Roads of Texas
Barns of California
Earl Thollander's Back Roads of California

Published by Clarkson N. Potter, Inc.,
225 Park Avenue South,
New York, New York 10003, and
represented in Canada by the
Canadian MANDA Group

CLARKSON N. POTTER, POTTER, and
colophon are trademarks of
Clarkson N. Potter, Inc.
Manufactured in the United States of America

Library of Congress Cataloging-in-Publication Data
Thollander, Earl.
Earl Thollander's San Francisco.
1. San Francisco (Calif.)—Description—Tours.
2. Walking—California—San Francisco—Guide-
books. I. Title.
F869.S33T46   1987    917.94'610453    86-25592
ISBN 0-517-56352-5

10 9 8 7 6 5 4 3 2 1
First Edition

"San Francisco has one drawback. 'Tis hard to leave."

RUDYARD KIPLING

Sancho Panza and Don Quixote, from the sculpture
in Golden Gate Park by Jo Mora

# Contents

*The Southwestern City*

*The South and Eastern City*

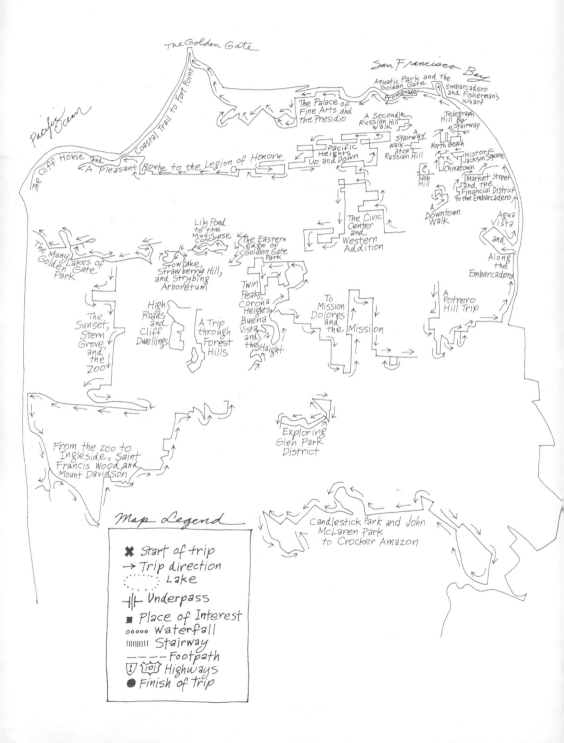

Map of all Trips

The Golden Gate

San Francisco Bay

Pacific Ocean

Aquatic Park and the Golden Gate Promenade

Embarcadero and Fisherman's Wharf

The Palace of Fine Arts and the Presidio

A Second Russian Hill Walk

Telegraph Hill by Stairway

Coastal Trail to Fort Point

A Stairway walk atop Russian Hill

North Beach

Historic Jackson Square

The Cliff House and A Pleasant Route to the Legion of Honore

Pacific Heights Up and Down

Chinatown

Nob Hill

Market Street and the Financial District to the Embarcadero

A Downtown Walk

Agua Vista and

The Civic Center and Western Addition

Along the Embarcadero

The Many Lakes of Golden Gate Park

Lily Pond to the Music Concourse

The Eastern Edge of Golden Gate Park

To Mission Dolores and the Mission

A Potrero Hill Trip

Stow Lake, Strawberry Hill, and Strybing Arboretum

Twin Peaks, Corona Heights, Buena Vista, and the Haight

The Sunset, Stern Grove, and the Zoo

High Roads and Cliff Dwellings

A Trip through Forest Hills

Exploring Glen Park District

From the Zoo to Ingleside, Saint Francis Wood and Mount Davidson

Map Legend

✗ Start of trip
→ Trip direction
Lake
Underpass
■ Place of Interest
ooooo Waterfall
Stairway
------ Footpath
Highways
● Finish of trip

Candlestick Park and John McLaren Park to Crocker Amazon

# Introduction

San Francisco is one of the most beautiful and fascinating cities in the world, yet there are sights and pleasures beyond the well-known landmarks which can easily be overlooked. The aim of this book, in addition to pointing out the landmarks, is to direct you to whatever is new or special, to acquaint you with out-of-the-way places of particular charm, to introduce you to neighborhoods that truly reflect the life and spirit of the city and its people.

I made my home in San Francisco for forty-some years and returned with renewed enthusiasm to research my book, exploring old haunts and seeking out the unusual. My routes, which took me up, down, around, and over most of the city's forty-seven-plus hills, are included in these pages. I hope you will find—as I did—that they make for a unique and unforgettable journey of discovery.

You can either walk, drive, jog, or bicycle along these routes. But stairways, of course, can only be walked, and parking a car can be a major problem in some areas. Public transportation may be a solution in many cases. Buses, trolleys, and streetcars are available to take you to or near your destination, anywhere in San Francisco.

For information about public transportation routes, the "San Francisco Street and Transit Map," published by the San Francisco Municipal Railway Community Affairs Department, is essential. You can purchase one at the San Francisco Visitors and Convention Bureau in Hallidie Plaza at Fifth and Market streets. You can also find out about the opening hours of museums and other attractions here. A map of the city, available at the Center, or at map stores, shops catering to tourists, and automobile club offices, is useful, too, as is the "Map & Guide to Golden Gate Park," published by Friends of Recreation and Parks and available at the Recreation and Parks Department, Fell and Stanyan streets in Golden Gate Park, or at the Visitor Information Center.

Now, on to San Francisco!

The Ferry Building, Bay Bridge, and Vaillencourt Fountain

Lotta's Fountain

# A Downtown Walk

This walk begins at Fifth and Mission streets, the site of the old San Francisco Mint. A solid example of Federal classical revival architecture, the mint was built for the ages back in 1874, and one-third of the nation's wealth in gold and bullion was stored here. Today, it serves as a museum among whose exhibits is a photograph showing the building standing strong amid the rubble of the 1906 earthquake; it was the only banking facility left in operation after the disaster. Also on display are coins and gold ingots, a miner's cabin, a five-stamp mill for crushing rock ore, and a photograph of famous opera star Madame Tetrazzini singing "The Last Rose of Summer" at Lotta's Fountain on Christmas Eve, 1910.

Hallidie Plaza at Market and Fifth streets was named after Andrew Hallidie, a Scotsman who in 1873 perfected and installed San Francisco's first cable cars. Situated one flight below the street, the Plaza has become a center for street performers, speakers, and demonstrators, and other activities and entertainments. This is also the location of the San Francisco Visitors and Convention Bureau where tourists can obtain brochures, maps, and sight-seeing advice.

As you walk east along Market Street you'll see an incredible parade of itinerants and city dwellers, from the seedy to the flamboyant. At Market and Powell you'll find the Bank of America, a fine example of Italian Renaissance-Baroque architecture. Cross Market at Powell and stroll into the Emporium-Capwell department store for a view of the great glass-roofed rotunda, then continue to Market and Grant where you'll see the small but elegant 1910 Wells Fargo Building.

The store at 140 Maiden Lane is the only Frank Lloyd Wright design in San Francisco. Like a cave, the building has but one entrance; its well-lit interior is circular.

Maiden Lane emerges on to Stockton Street. Directly ahead there is a view of Union Square and its 1901 memorial shaft saluting Admiral Dewey's capture of Manila from the Spanish in 1898. Behind the monument and beyond the Square is the St. Francis Hotel, one of the city's great hostelries.

Sutter

450

Ruth asawa sculpture

Post

Frank Lloyd Wright design

Kearny

St. Francis Hotel

Union Square

Maiden Lane

Lottie's Fountain

Geary

nieman Marcus

O'Farrell

Stockton

Geary

Wells Fargo

Market Street

Ellis

Cyril Magnin

Powell (cable car)

Mason

a Downtown Walk (1 mile)

Eddy

Bank of america

The Emporium

4th St.

San Francisco and Convention

Visitor Bureau (Hallidie Plaza)

Jessie

stevenson

Old Mint

Mission St.

Parking Area

5th St.

14

On the west side of Stockton Street between Sutter and Post streets, you'll discover a fountain designed by sculptor Ruth Asawa honoring San Francisco's bridges, hills, and architecture. It is detailed with amusing figures, fish, frogs, monsters, and other creatures.

Continue up Stockton Street to Sutter, turn left and you'll soon come to 450 Sutter Street, said to be one of the best examples of an Art Deco office building in the United States. Built during the Depression, when times were hard all over the country, this 1930 skyscraper proved to be San Francisco's last for two decades.

Between Post and Geary you might want to stop in at the 1907 St. Francis Hotel for a look at the massive black marble columns in the lobby and the fancy woodwork of the Compass Rose Room.

The park in front of the hotel is a pleasant place to sit and relax, watch the pigeons and the people, eat lunch, lie on the grass, or just meditate.

Outdoor flower stalls lend particular interest and color to this area.

At Stockton and Geary, the old City of Paris, now Nieman-Marcus, was modeled after turn-of-the-century Parisian department stores. Just inside the entrance, look up at the large dome of stained glass that brilliantly lights the interior. Every Christmas the space below it is occupied by a gigantic, wonderfully decorated tree.

# Market Street and the Financial District to the Embarcadero

On its little concrete island at Kearny and Market streets, Lotta's Fountain memorializes Luisa Tetrazzini, the famous opera star who made her American debut in San Francisco at the turn of the century. The sculpture was presented to the citizens of the city in 1875 by actress Lotta Crabtree, once the rage of San Francisco's music halls. The plaque honoring the opera star was added many years later. Its message reads, "To

16

Embarcadero Plaza — Ferry Bldg.
Justin Herman Plaza
Drumm
Hyatt Regency
Cable car terminal

Market Street and the Financial District to the Embarcadero (1 mile)

remember Christmas Eve, 1910, when Luisa Tetrazzini sang to the people of San Francisco on this spot."

The building on the southeast corner of Market and Third streets marks the site where, in 1887, William Randolph Hearst began his newspaper publishing career. Diagonally opposite is a French Renaissance–inspired 1902 office building—now housing First Nationwide Savings— that withstood the 1906 earthquake and fire.

At New Montgomery and Market the Sheraton Palace Hotel still boasts one of the grandest dining rooms of old San Francisco. The Hobart Building at 582 Market was designed by the eminent architect Willis Polk, who was responsible for a goodly number of distinguished buildings and dwellings of pre- and post-earthquake San Francisco. The tower of this 1914 structure is rich with ornate detail.

If you walk through Crocker Galleria, mid-block between Post and Sutter, you'll come directly upon another Willis Polk design, the famous Hallidie Building at 130 Sutter Street. A completely glass-fronted office building, such as this one, was regarded as an architectural freak back in 1917. Nevertheless, it opened the door to a new and imaginative idea that really didn't catch on until many years later.

17

From the north corner of Sutter and Montgomery, look back up Sutter past Crocker Galleria to see, painted on the side of a building, the gigantic *trompe l'oeil* towel blowing in the wind.

At 220 Montgomery is the Mills Building, with its intricately carved, massive, arched entrance, and at 100 Bush stands the zigzag-design Art Deco 1930 Shell Oil Building. The Crown Zellerbach Building near Bush and Market streets heralded the office building boom of the 1960s. Mascarini's sculpture in the lobby and David Tolerton's splashing fountain outside lift the spirits with their expression of freedom, lightness, and motion. The World of Oil Museum and the Chevron Art Gallery are across the street at 555 Market.

West of Zellerbach, on Sutter, you'll come upon a delightful enclosed plaza where trees emerge as if by magic from a marble floor. Here, too, is a delightful fountain. Number 130 Bush, designed by George Applegarth in 1910, must be San Francisco's narrowest skyscraper—just twenty feet wide! "Progress of Man," the 1930 Art Deco sculptures by Ralph Stackpole, sit solidly on each side of the steps of the classic Pacific Stock Exchange at 155 Sansome.

The Royal Insurance Building, 201 Sansome, has five marble doorways from the dismantled Torlonia Palace (1680) of Rome. One is at the entrance and four are directly inside. Another Willis Polk design, the 1903 Merchants Exchange at 465 California Street, boasts fine murals inside by William Coulter, a foremost maritime artist of the time. There are also excellent ship models on display, including one of the *Gjöa,* the ship Roald Amundsen sailed to the Northwest Passage.

Enter the Wells Fargo History Room at 420 Montgomery Street to see an excellent exhibit of California historical material. Following this go through the bank, exiting at 464 California Street. In front of the building, near Leidesdorff, there is a historic iron hitching post. Inside the decorative post is a storage chamber that once held nosebags of barley for patrons' horses.

The Bank of California, at 400 California Street, was built in 1908 and is a city landmark. Its facade is of Tennessee marble. One wall of its spacious interior is graced by a clock topped with marble lions by Arthur Putnam, a famous animal sculptor of the time. Down one flight of stairs you'll find the fascinating Museum of Money of the American West.

At 350 California a fine marble frame of curved walrus heads is all that is left of the 1908 Alaska Commercial Building, disassembled in 1975.

You might want to stop in at the Hyatt Regency Hotel for a look around. People and objects look like mere toys in an immense fairyland setting.

Justin Herman Plaza is the place to see Jean Dubuffet's charming stainless steel *Le Chiffonière* and to watch Armand Vallaincourt's bulky fountain do what it does.

Along this downtown walk you'll note the great variety of people who make up the city. I recall especially the day I was here when a street musician played the cimbalom (a Hungarian instrument also known as a gypsy dulcimer) for me, and a large, noisy parade of goofily costumed people reminded me that it was, after all, April 1, the day of tolerance toward the incongruous.

# Chinatown

San Francisco had its beginnings right here in what is now the Portsmouth Square area of Chinatown. A tiny wall plaque at 823 Grant Avenue marks the site of the first habitation, a shanty of rough boards built in 1837 by sea captain William Richardson. Later, Portsmouth Square was the plaza of the Spanish town of Yerba Buena.

At Portsmouth Square you can watch Chinatown's residents playing cards or chess, read the Robert Louis Stevenson memorial, or feed the pigeons that cluster near the Mary Fuller–Robert McChesney sculptural area for small children. A short walk away across the footbridge over Kearny Street, you'll find the Chinese Culture Foundation (open Tuesday through Saturday, 1–4 P.M.), where you can see an exhibit of Chinese fine art and learn of the activities of the Center.

Walk up Washington Street and note Sam Wo's, perhaps the narrowest three-story restaurant in San Francisco. In one of the stores along here you might count, as I did, some forty-two barbecued ducks hanging in the window. Along Ross take a peek into the factory rooms filled with women stitching and sewing and chattering gaily as they work, and at 56 Ross watch fortune cookies in the making. On Jason, visit the underground aquarium.

Along Jackson are bakeries, and herb, spice, and tea shops emitting exotic aromas into the narrow street, while along Stockton grocery stores and other shops stocked to their ceilings offer unusual products from China.

On Washington again, turn into Old Chinatown Lane where there are more tiny garment factories.

*Sun Yat Sen by Bufano and Old St. Mary's Church in Chinatown*

At 125 Waverly you can mount the stairs to Tin How (also written "T'ien Hou") Temple. The steep climb is rewarding, for the interior is rich in color and detail. The day I was here oranges were in abundance, a symbolic wish for prosperity, I was told. Incense burned all around, even on the open balcony where the sweet smell wafted over Chinatown.

At 109 Waverly another flight of stairs leads to Norras Temple. It was here that I came upon a monk in a yellow robe drawing an intricate religious design on paper, to be used for wall decoration.

The colorful building at 843 Stockton is that of Chinese Six Companies. Another temple can be found at 855 Stockton. When I was here, at Kong Chow Temple, I learned that I could receive a prediction of the future for a small fee. I was first asked my occupation. I answered that I was working on a book. Then I was asked to pick a bamboo stick from a tubular bamboo container. The number on the stick corresponded to predictions printed on various pieces of paper fastened to the wall. With my number selected and the corresponding prediction in hand, I was seated with an elderly gentleman who explained the four lines of Chinese characters. The first line was translated to say that I was working on a book. The second line said that it would be successful. The third said, of course, that I would make lots of money. The last nicely rounded out the prediction by saying that I would also be healthy and happy. Perhaps your prediction will be equally optimistic. Such a soul-warming experience costs but two dollars.

When you leave the temple walk along the west side of Stockton Street to see the markets and the shopping activity, then stroll down Pacific to Grant, a street of colorful fish markets. At 17 Adler Street visit the Chinese Historical Society's museum (open Tuesday through Saturday, 1–5 P.M.), where there is an excellent display of early photographs. Also on view are items as diverse as an authentic Chinese queue and a facsimile of a dragon's head, made in 1911 for parades.

There is another fine museum of Chinese immigrant history at 608 Commercial Street, sponsored by the Bank of Canton.

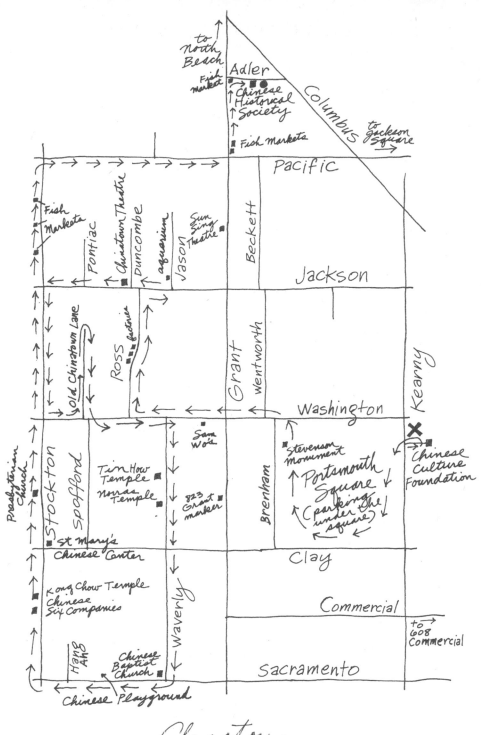

to
North
Beach

Fish
market

Adler

Columbus

to
Jackson
Square

Chinese
Historical
Society

Fish markets

Pacific

Fish
Markets

Pontiac

Chinatown Theatre

Duncombe

aquarium

Jason

Sun
Sing
Theatre

Beckett

Jackson

Old Chinatown Lane

Ross

Codinc

Grant

Wentworth

Washington

Presbyterian Church

Stockton

Spofford

Tin How
Temple

Norras
Temple

Sam
Wo's

823
Grant
marker

Brenham

Stevenson
monument

Portsmouth
Square

(parking
under the
square)

X

Chinese
Culture
Foundation

Kearny

St Mary's
Chinese Center

Clay

Kong Chow Temple
Chinese
Six Companies

Waverly

Commercial

to
608
Commercial

Hang
Ahs

Chinese
Baptist
Church

Sacramento

Chinese Playground

*Chinatown*

(1 mile)

*North Beach*

As a young San Francisco artist I did a painting from the same location in Washington Square that is shown in the illustration on pages 26–27. The great cypress is even more magnificent today, an ideal foil for the straight, simple lines of Coit Tower. People enjoy exercising, playing guitars, walking, or just sitting in this engaging place.

The Washington Square statue of three fishermen and a rescued damsel, dedicated to the 1846–1866 Volunteer Fire Department of San Francisco, was bequeathed by Lillie Hitchcock Coit, colorful heiress and enthusiastic chaser of fire wagons. The rest of her bequest went to build Coit Tower.

The other statue, in the middle of the park, is of Benjamin Franklin. Carved in the base is the cheerless message, "Presented by H. D. Cogswell to our boys and girls who will soon take our places and pass on." Cogswell was a wealthy dentist who also erected statues of himself, none of which remain.

The building at 1736 Stockton, just off the Square, was designed by Bernard Maybeck, one of the West's most distinguished architects, in 1907.

A zigzag route through the streets that cling to Telegraph Hill is the most interesting one to take. Some of the streets are narrow and exude the atmosphere of early San Francisco. Along Sonoma Street balconies pattern the flat-fronted old houses.

On Castle Street trees grow where there is no room for trees! From 287 Union to the corner of Montgomery are four charming dwellings of varied designs from the late 1800s.

Walk along the upper terrace of Calhoun to the end. There is a precipice here that affords a dramatic Embarcadero and downtown view. A 1939 house, designed in the spare international style by Viennese-trained architect Richard Neutra, is just below at number 66 on split-level Calhoun Terrace. Number 9 Calhoun is a San Francisco cottage of the 1850s, and the house at 31 Alta Street, off Montgomery, is also very old, having a construction date of 1852!

Since 1922, Julius Castle Restaurant has clung precariously to its cliff at the end of Montgomery Street. It once had a turntable for cars because there was no way to turn around at this point in the old days. (It is still difficult!)

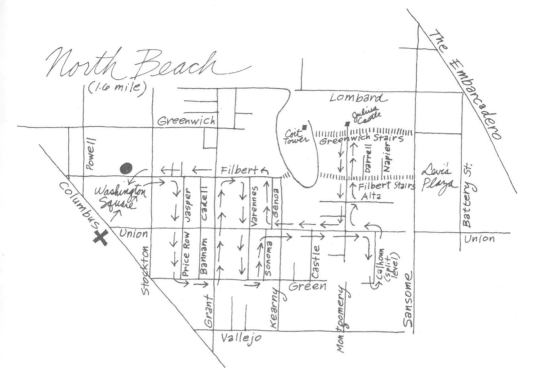

North Beach
(1.6 mile)

Telegraph Hill by Stairway

Levi's Plaza at the end of Filbert has a "walk-through fountain" and there are trees, lawns, and places to sit along the Embarcadero here.

The Greenwich stairs lead up to Coit Tower from Filbert Street. There are also stairs down to Filbert on the opposite side of Telegraph Hill. If you decide to take the formidable stairway all the way to the top, leave yourself enough time to go slowly. The first bench you'll reach has a small inscription reading, "I have a feeling we're not in Kansas anymore." The day I made my climb, several house owners along the way were out pruning trees. I asked one of them if he minded people gawking at his house and garden. He smiled and said, "No, not really." Homeowners obviously take pride in creating admirable gardens along the stairway.

Early San Francisco wooden houses on both Darrell Place and Napier Lane, off the Filbert Street stairs, offer quaint exteriors harking back to Gold Rush days.

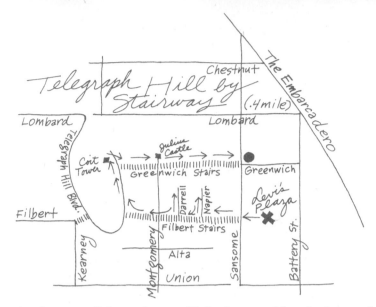

Telegraph Hill by Stairway (.4mile)

Chestnut

The Embarcadero

Lombard

Lombard

Telegraph Hill Blvd.

Coit Tower

Julius Castle

Greenwich Stairs

Greenwich

Levi's Plaza

Filbert

Darrell

Napier

Filbert Stairs

Kearney

Montgomery

Alta

Union

Sansome

Battery St.

At the top of the stairs you'll find yourself at the base of Coit Tower. If you go at the end of the day, you may be fortunate enough, as I was, to view a glowing sunset behind the Golden Gate Bridge at the same time a full moon is rising to the east. The beauty at such a moment is breathtaking.

Coit Tower, completed in 1933, stands where the inner harbor signal stood in the 1840s and 1850s. It was Lillie Coit's idea to build this tower both in memory of her husband and to honor the volunteer firemen of the city. The work of San Francisco artists on the walls of the tower is an evocation of the thirties.

Coit Tower and Telegraph Hill from Washington Square

# Historic Jackson Square

Jackson Square, where a number of downtown buildings survived the 1906 earthquake and fire, was San Francisco's first designated Historic District. An 1877 Italianate firehouse stands at 441–451 Pacific. Number 555, built in 1907, was formerly a dance hall, and number 580 was the only Barbary Coast saloon to survive the 1906 disaster. It was known as "Diana's."

At Columbus and Kearny you'll see a 1911 classical revival "flatiron"-style building that once housed the old Fugazi Bank, officially called Banca Operaia Italiana Fugazi. Abe Ruef, a political boss of the twenties, had offices there in 1915 following his incarceration in San Quentin Penitentiary.

Along Montgomery Street, at 722–728, is the Belli Building, constructed in the early 1850s to house a local merchant's chinaware business. The Golden Era Building, at 730–732, was once the headquarters of the *Golden Era Periodical,* which published articles by such names as Bret Harte, Mark Twain, and Thomas Starr King during the 1850s and 1860s.

The bank at 498 Jackson was established in 1854 by William Tecumseh Sherman, the famous Civil War general who had previously been a banker in San Francisco. The building at 451, with its alternating pointed and arched window pediments, served as a liquor warehouse for a Mr. Hotaling in 1866. Another of his warehouses, built in 1860, stands at 463.

The building at 432–436 Jackson dates back to 1865 and formerly housed the French Consulate. In 1857, number 472 was the first site of the Ghirardelli Chocolate Factory before it moved to its later location near Aquatic Park. Nearby Balance Street was named for a cargo ship called the *Balance.* Like so many other ships, it had been abandoned by its gold-seeking officers and crew during the Gold Rush. It eventually became engulfed, built over and incorporated as part of a wharf at this very spot. There is no longer any sign of ship or wharf.

Hotaling Street leads to Transamerica Corporation's "Redwood Park" and sculpture garden. Here, you can admire the flourishing redwood trees and contemplate the soaring point of Transamerica Pyramid, the tallest of San Francisco's buildings.

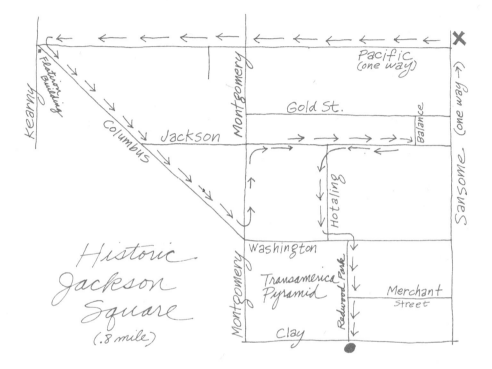

# Embarcadero and Fisherman's Wharf

An embarcadero is a landing place, and San Francisco's inner shoreline truly is just that. Wares from all over the world are brought here by ships of all nations. This is one of the city's water boundaries, this eastern edge along the bay replete with piers, wharves, shipping, gulls, and the smell of the sea.

In the marina between piers 35 and 39 is a glistening metal sculpture called *Skygate,* by Roger Barr.

Investigate Pier 39's many restaurants and amusements, but also circle around the outside rim of the pier. There are good boat and bay views and Alcatraz Island seems at its closest to shore here.

At Pier 41 reservations can be made to visit famed Alcatraz, Island of the Pelicans. Actually, Yerba Buena Island was the real Pelican Island. An early survey map had mistaken one island for the other. With brown pelicans now nesting on Alcatraz, however, the name finally fits. In 1933, the island also became known as "The Rock," site of the formidable prison that once held the likes of such folks as mobster Al Capone and "Machine Gun" Kelly.

A square-rigged sailing ship, the *Balclutha,* open to visitors for a small fee, is docked at Pier 43—or was at the time of this writing. It was launched in Scotland in 1886 and

Mt. Tamalpais, San Francisco Bay, and Alcatraz

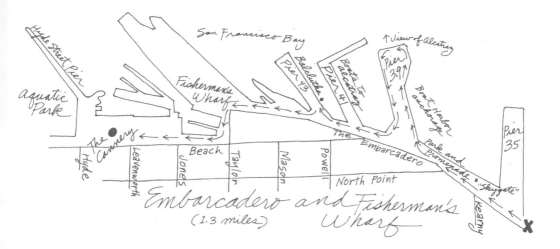

San Francisco Bay

Hyde Street Pier

Aquatic Park

Fisherman's Wharf

Balclutha Pier 43

Boats to Alcatraz Pier 41

↑ View of Alcatraz

Pier 39

Boat Harbor anchorage

The Cannery

The Embarcadero

Park and Promenade  "Skygate"

Pier 35

Hyde · Leavenworth · Jones · Taylor · Mason · Powell

Beach

North Point

Embarcadero and Fisherman's Wharf

(1.3 miles)

Chestnut

has to its credit seventeen turns around Cape Horn as a cargo ship. There is a plan to one day move it to Aquatic Park, where other historic ships are moored.

Behind the clutter and crush of the restaurant and souvenir trade at Fisherman's Wharf, little crab-fishing boats sit quietly moored beside one another. These boats leave as early as 3 A.M. in the fishing season to collect their catch from and to rebait the crab nets and pots along the Pacific coast.

From Fisherman's Wharf you can stroll to the cannery for a look at its many interesting shops.

*Nob Hill*

You can ride the cable car from Powell and Market streets up the steep hills to the top of Nob Hill at Powell and California. The elegant brick building at 800 Powell houses the University Club, a prestigious men's club that is some hundred years old. The building itself was constructed soon after the 1906 earthquake and fire.

Stanford Court (1909), remodeled and turned into a hotel in 1972, is located at California and Powell on the former site of Leland Stanford's stables. The wealthy and influential Stanford founded Stanford University in Palo Alto in memory of his son, who died at age fifteen.

Mason and California, where the Mark Hopkins Art Institute stood until it was destroyed in the 1906 fire, now is the site of the 1925 Mark Hopkins Hotel. The Top of the Mark, which is open after 4 P.M. daily, opened in 1939 and was the first cocktail lounge to offer patrons an awe-inspiring view of the city along with their favorite drinks.

Across from the Mark Hopkins, all in a row from 831 to 849 Mason Street, are four town houses designed in 1917 by Willis Polk, a prominent architect of his day. Polk's work is worth noting for its simple elegance and individuality.

Stop in at the Fairmont Hotel, an Italian Renaissance design by architect Stanford White. (Many years ago, here in the lobby, I chanced upon the surrealist painter Salvador Dali. I still carry the image in my mind of a tall figure dressed in black, his expression somber and austere behind an elegant black mustache.) If you walk left and to the rear of the hotel you can take the sky-lift elevator to the elegant Crown Room for a cocktail and a view. The ride is particularly eerie if you look straight down. Don't do that. Simply look out at the marvelous expanding view.

At 1001 California is a French baroque-style apartment house. The town house at 1021, which dates from 1911, looks small for its location—only two stories high—but it is five stories high in the rear! The Pacific Union Club building (1000 California) was originally constructed in 1886 as a home for the James Flood family, and is the only Nob Hill mansion to survive the 1906 earthquake and fire. Ornate in style, it has forty-two rooms and now serves as a private clubhouse.

Huntington Park, bequeathed to the city in 1915 by the widow of railroad tycoon Collis P. Huntington, is a well-kept bit of greenery where Chinese women sometimes meet to perform the graceful exercises of T'ai Chi Ch'uan. The delightful marble fountain here, a copy of an Italian design, is carved with figures hoisting turtles and cavorting with dolphins.

Grace Cathedral has aspects of Chartres, Amiens, and Notre Dame. Its "Singing Tower" has forty-four bells, of which the bourdon, the largest bell of its kind in the West, rings the hour. The cathedral's Lorenzo Ghiberti doors, with scenes from the Old Testament, were cast from the same molds as his "Doors of Paradise" on the baptistery of San Giovanni in Florence. The murals inside the church were painted by John DeRosen and the late Antonio Sotomayor.

The Fountain in Huntington Park and Grace Cathedral

The grounds were given to the Episcopal Diocese of California by the family of railroad magnate Charles Crocker whose two mansions had been destroyed here in 1906.

Opposite Grace Cathedral stop in at the Masonic Auditorium for a look at its gigantic—forty-five feet wide by forty-eight feet high—glass mural, which depicts the history of California masonry. The mural is also of interest for the way it was fabricated of thousands of bits of metal, parchment, felt, linen, silk, natural foliage, thinly sliced vegetable matter, shells and other objects from the sea, and pieces of stained glass in 180 colors.

At 1110 Taylor Street is a pre-earthquake classical revival cottage supposedly built for James Flood's coachman.

The Cable Car Museum is at Mason and Washington streets. This is more than a museum, however, with its "winding machinery" working at full tilt; twenty-seven cable cars may be in use at any one time. In the Sheave Room downstairs you'll see the cables working their way under Mason and Washington streets.

# A Stairway Walk atop Russian Hill

If you debark from the cable car at Mason and Vallejo streets you can hike up Russian Hill on the Vallejo Street stairs. Ina Coolbrith, a poet and librarian and one of Russian Hill's most notable residents, lived here, and the small park at the top of the stairs is dedicated to her memory. She had helped Jack London in his career, and Bret Harte is said to have wanted to marry her. Willis Polk, the famous San Francisco architect, lived in the 1892 brown shingle house at 1015–1019 Vallejo Street.

Along Florence Street are brown, tan, and pink stuccoed houses, their surfaces unadorned except for exposed outer beams, hinting of Southwest Mission architecture. At the end of Florence, down the steps and to the left, at number 1032, is one of San Francisco's oldest dwellings (1853), known as Atkinson House. Painted a rich gray, it sits serenely in its lovely, wooded garden on the steep slope of Russian Hill.

An abundance of pre-earthquake homes can be found in the 1000 block of Green Street, including a former firehouse at 1088 and the Fusier Octagon House at 1067.

Macondray Lane is resplendent in cool greenery, which sets off the extravagant pink blossoms of rhododendrons in spring. At the end of Macondray you'll be just two blocks from the Mason Street cable car.

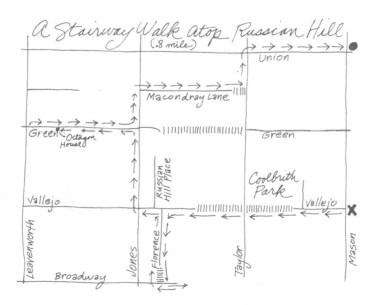

A Stairway Walk atop Russian Hill (.8 mile)

# A Second Russian Hill Walk

You can swing off the Powell–Hyde Street cable car at Hyde and Greenwich streets. On the southwest corner you'll see the tall apartment building that was featured in *Dark Passage,* a movie starring Humphrey Bogart, which was based on the book by Dashiell Hammett. Hammett himself lived at 1309 Hyde Street.

Walk up the brick road to see the attractive Alice Marble Tennis Courts named for the famous tennis pro of the 1930s. The park next to it is dedicated to poet George Sterling, who lived on Russian Hill at the turn of the century.

As you walk one block to Lombard you will hear the underground Hyde Street trolley cables humming their one-note tune. Lombard Street's picturesque one-way brick road twists left and right eight times to Leavenworth Street. Descend the stairs and turn left on Leavenworth, then right on Chestnut. Here you'll find the Spanish Colonial Revival building that houses the San Francisco Art Institute (where I was once a student). When you enter, go left to the Diego Rivera Gallery where you'll see a fresco painted by the great

*Cable Car ascending the Hyde Street Hill*

36

Map labels:
North Point
To Ghirardelli Square
Russian Hill Park
Bay
a Second Russian
Francisco
Hill Walk (.7 mile)
The Art Institute
Hyde
Chestnut
Leavenworth
Jones
Lombard
George Sterling Park
alice marble Tennis Courts
Greenwich

Mexican muralist in 1931, and in which he prominently immortalized his broad backside. The works exhibited in this gallery and in the Emmanuel Walter and Atholl McBean galleries in the new wing of the institute are stimulating and provocative.

Emerge from the institute onto Francisco Street and turn left. The house at 825 Francisco Street was built in 1849 and is one of the very oldest in the city. Its handsome Italianate exterior was added later. Turning right at 2540–2550 Hyde you'll see a row of elegant cottages. From this side of the street, take a look across at number 2626, an 1850s house that was beautifully remodeled in 1954 by the great landscape architect Thomas Church. Now, you are within easy walking distance to the Cannery, Ghirardelli Square, the Hyde Street Pier, and more.

# Aquatic Park and the Golden Gate Promenade

The cable car comes down the long Hyde Street hill, ending its journey at Victorian Park. This is the eastern end of the Golden Gate National Recreation Area where you'll find the Cannery. Designed like an open-air marketplace, it was originally used by Del Monte Fruit Company.

Historic ships are moored and anchored off Hyde Street Pier. The *Eppleton Hall,* shown in my drawing, is a 1914 side-wheel tugboat brought from Newcastle, England, through the efforts of Karl Kortum, director of the National Maritime Museum, and Scott Newhall, who wrote a book about the voyage called *The Eppleton Hall.*

Nearby is Ghirardelli Square, a marvelous jumble of mostly old brick structures pleasingly arranged into shops and restaurants.

The Maritime Museum originally was a bathhouse built in "Streamlined Art Moderne" nautical style in 1939. It later

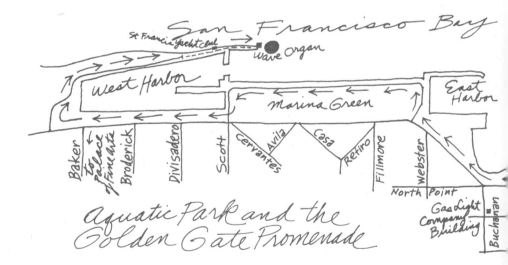

Aquatic Park and the Golden Gate Promenade

became a casino and, finally, a "white elephant" until 1951 when it became the Maritime Museum. Perhaps someday the building will be a bathhouse again, for the museum's collection is too large for it and is scheduled to move to the Haslett Warehouse on Hyde Street.

The waters surrounding Aquatic Park are too cold for swimming but there are many hardy souls who do. When I watched some of them from the bleachers recently I was reminded of the day when a friend and I swam across those waters to the faraway end of the Municipal Pier. We were almost swept out into the Bay by undercurrents but eventually reached the pier ladder and were hauled to safety.

Near the Maritime Museum are public bocce ball courts, the Italian version of lawn bowling. You might want to try your hand at it.

You should walk from Aquatic Park to Fort Mason. This wooded point of land was first settled in the 1950s by many notable citizens, including John C. Frémont, explorer and geographer of the West. His house was later torn down to make way for fortifications.

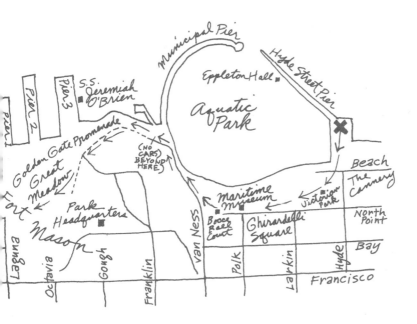

At Pier 3, the Liberty ship SS *Jeremiah O'Brien* is open to the public daily. It is the last of the unaltered World War II Liberty ships, still in operating condition but now used only as a museum. Nearby is Park Headquarters where Golden Gate National Recreation Area information can be obtained.

Fort Mason Center is a cultural center housing a great many nonprofit organizations serving community needs. Museo Italo Americano, a museum featuring Italian-American art, culture, and history, can be found here in Building C.

The Golden Gate Promenade goes from Aquatic Park through Marina Green, with places to stop and exercise if you wish. Various exercises are described at each of eighteen

The Paddle-Wheeler tug,
Eppleton Hall,
Hyde Street Pier

stations. Beyond the Saint Francis Yacht Club, at the end of the jetty created by Yacht Harbor, is the Wave Organ. You can park nearby and walk to the very end of the promontory to see and hear it. You will find a tiny stone park designed from discarded granite curbing and old tombstones, an inspired work of stone masonry and an entertaining piece of public art. At high tide subtle gurglings and flushing sounds emanate from pipes and holes designed to pick up the music of the sea. At low tide the park is also a pleasant place to sit, but then the Wave Organ is quiet. The Promenade continues past West Harbor and all the way to historic Fort Point. It is a hiking or jogging trail accessible at any point to anyone.

The Old Washington Street Firehouse

## Pacific Heights Up and Down

You'll have to go up and down this way and that to see the great collection of wonderful homes in Pacific Heights. I planned the route this way so that you can take advantage of some of the most beautiful and picturesque streets in the area.

Start your tour at 1990 California Street, a huge house combining many styles of Victorian design. Then continue on to 2355 Washington Street, a three-story 1882 Italianate house that was the residence of the daughter of Adolph Sutro. She was one of the first women to practice medicine in the nineteenth century. Her father, known as the Great Engineer, made a fortune digging a tunnel for miners through the Comstock Lode in Nevada. He also did a stint as mayor of San Francisco from 1894 to 1896.

Number 2373 is a gaily painted Carpenter Gothic house built in 1888, and 2209, which dates from 1861, has a picket fence with roses.

The massive red sandstone Whittier Mansion at 2090 Jackson Street is the headquarters of the California Historical Society. It was built so solidly in the 1890s that only a chimney toppled over during the 1906 earthquake. The house is open to the public Wednesday, Saturday, and Sunday, 1–5 P.M.

The 1912 mansion of sugar king Adolph Spreckels, at 2080 Washington Street, was designed to resemble a French palace and takes up much of the block. The Haas-Lilienthal House at 2007 Franklin Street is an excellent example, inside and out, of the opulent architecture of 1886. It is open for tours on Wednesdays and Sundays. Number 1772 Vallejo is a handsome Victorian home with a mansard roof, and the house at 1815 Vallejo is notable for its arrangement of windows of various sizes.

The Octagon House at 2645 Gough Street was built in 1857. Eight-sided houses, the owners believed, brought good luck. This one is open to the public every second and fourth Thursday, and every second Sunday from 1–3 P.M. Holy Trinity Cathedral, at 1520 Green Street, was built in 1908 and is a classical adaptation of Russian church architecture. The biggest of the seven bells in its belfry was crafted in Moscow in 1888 and was a gift from Czar Alexander III.

The Alhambra Theatre (Polk between Union and Green streets) is San Francisco's Moorish-style movie house, complete with minarets; and the 1905 mansion at Filbert and Webster, which houses the orthodox Hindu Philosophic Vedanta Society, displays a most unusual combination of Queen Anne, Colonial, Medieval, and Oriental architecture.

A series of flats, built in 1875 at 1950–1960 Green, were moved in 1891, and in consequence the facades became reversed, with balustraded balconies where the back doors were once in view. One can only guess why such a curious move was made. The house at 2160 Green Street was built in 1879 for Leander P. Sherman of Sherman Clay Music Company. Paderewski, Madame Schumann-Heink, and Lotta Crabtree performed in its music room.

St. Vincent de Paul Church (1916) blocks off the street, when necessary, at Green and Steiner so that the children attending their school can use it as a playground during recess. Inside the church the stained-glass windows cast a jewellike glow.

An artesian well can be seen in the courtyard of the 1891 St. Mary the Virgin Episcopal Church at 2301 Union Street. Number 2460 is a handsome Victorian home (1872), with a mansard roof and twin dormers.

The trip down Green Street, off Scott, is rather exciting— it is so steep! On Pierce, number 2727 is the Casebolt House, named for its former owners and one of the oldest houses here, dating from 1865 when it was a farmhouse in a meadow then called Cow Hollow. Huge ship timbers support its four sides.

In contrast to San Francisco's Victorians is Howard House, at 2944 Jackson Street, built in the streamlined Art Moderne style of 1939.

The design for the Church of the New Jerusalem at 2107 Lyon Street was inspired by artist Bruce Porter's sketches of an Italian village church. Reverend Worcester of the church, artist William Keith, and architects A. Page Brown and A. Schweinfurth collaborated on the final design. Bernard Maybeck, who later was to design the Palace of Fine Arts, to this day one of San Francisco's most revered buildings, worked in A. Page Brown's architectural firm in the 1890s,

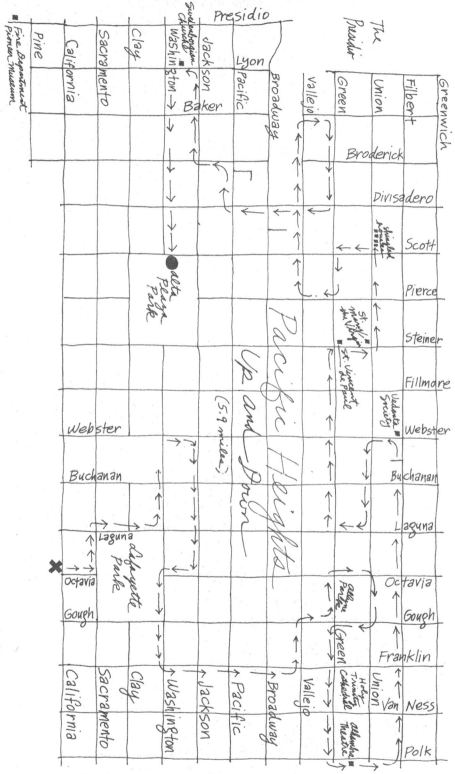

and apparently it was his idea to use the madrone tree trunk arches that still grace the interior of the church. William Keith painted the pictures hanging on the north wall that depict the changing of California's seasons, and Bruce Porter designed the little stained-glass windows.

The house at 3022 Washington Street, pictured on page 40, was once a Victorian firehouse.

Alta Plaza Park, with its greenery and broad views of the city, is a good place to stop and rest. Seven row houses (2637–2673), which can be seen below on Clay Street, are Italianate in style and date from 1875.

Not on the tour but a place of interest you might want to visit in the vicinity at Presidio and Pine, is the San Francisco Fire Department Pioneer Memorial Museum, open 1–4 P.M., Thursday through Sunday.

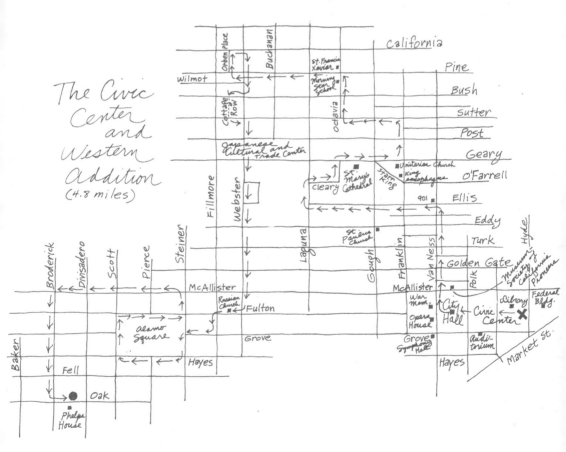

# The Civic Center and Western Addition

Daniel Burnham, architect, city planner, and designer of the World's Columbian Exposition of 1893 in Chicago, was commissioned by the city fathers several years before the earthquake and fire to beautify San Francisco. His plan was like a smaller version of the grand design of Paris. After so much was destroyed in the 1906 disaster, the time seemed right to implement his ideas. Instead, politics and public apathy toward the cost of beautification resulted in the cancellation of almost all of Burnham's plan except for his Civic Center.

The City Hall, designed by San Francisco architects Arthur Brown, Jr., and John Bakewell, Jr., and dedicated on December 29, 1915, is impressive, imposing, and aesthetically pleasing. From its eastern steps you can see flags and fountains and a sweeping view to faraway United Nations Plaza. The 1914 Civic Auditorium is to the right as you look east and the Public Library is ahead and to the left. West of City Hall are the Opera House, Symphony Hall, and the Veterans' War Memorial Building, which houses the San Francisco Museum of Modern Art.

The Museum of the Society of California Pioneers, at 456 McAllister, has a fine collection of photographs of old San Francisco among many other items of interest. The museum is open 10 A.M.–4 P.M., Monday through Friday.

At 901 Van Ness Avenue a showroom designed by Bernard Maybeck and constructed in 1926 displays prestigious automobiles.

Saint Mary's Cathedral, 1971, on Geary between Laguna and Gough, astonishes first-time visitors with the immensity of its interior. A canopy by sculptor Robert Lippold, made from seemingly thousands of aluminum rods, is suspended over the altar. Air currents move the rods, causing them to shimmer when the light is right.

Not on the tour, but standing clear on the horizon at the busy corner at Gough and Eddy, is the wooden 1894 Saint Paulus Church, whose design was inspired by Notre Dame Cathedral in Chartres. The church served as an emergency center for victims of the 1906 earthquake.

47

The 1888 First Unitarian Church at Franklin and Geary, a Romanesque Revival design, has many attractive additions to the original structure: meeting rooms, offices, schoolrooms, a chapel, and gallery space. Although modern in design, they all meld well with the old church. The sarcophagus of Thomas Starr King, humanitarian and apostle of liberty, is at the corner of Franklin and O'Farrell.

At 1409 Sutter you'll see an 1880 Stick-Eastlake-style Victorian house with a corner tower that resembles a candle-snuffer. Western Stick-style houses, so called because of the use of wooden sticks or strips to outline the bay windows, doors, and framework, were distinguished for their square bay windows, flat roof lines, and angular battens and decorations. With the addition of gingerbread millwork to their facades, these Victorian homes became known as Stick-Eastlake, after designer Charles Eastlake, who was credited with the idea for the new ornamentation. On the heels of Stick-Eastlake came the Queen Anne Victorian style with its steep gabled roofs, shingled walls or panels, a rounded turret or two, and a front porch inside the main structural frame.

*The City Hall*

Burt Orben, a local resident, in recent years worked so hard refurbishing houses along his street (between Pine and California on Webster) that neighbors helped get its name changed from Middle Place to Orben Place.

The Japanese Cultural and Trade Center, three blocks south, is a fascinating concentration of things Oriental, everything from saki and sushi to cherry trees, a torii (gate), and the Peace Pagoda.

The 900 block of Grove Street has a number of well-preserved old houses to admire: 926 (circa 1895), 957, and 975 (circa 1880). Along Steiner, from numbers 712 to 722, you'll find San Francisco's most photographed row of Victorian-style houses, built in 1894 and 1895 by Matthew Kavanaugh, a local carpenter with architectural savvy.

At 1198 Fulton is the 1889 villa called Westerfield House, a towered Victorian resembling lumber magnate William Carson's famous house in Eureka, California. Diagonally across the street, at 1201 Fulton, is a house of contrasting style designed by Arthur Brown, Jr., the architect who designed Coit Tower. On Steiner, number 908 is a much detailed Stick-style house built in 1899.

The handsome house at 1347 McAllister is châteauesque with baroque embellishments and oval windows.

The Abner Phelps house, set back near the middle of the block (between Broderick and Divisadero) and seen from Oak Street near Divisadero, may well be the oldest house intact in San Francisco. A Louisiana-style farmhouse, built perhaps between 1850 and 1860, it was prefabricated in New Orleans and transported to San Francisco by ship around Cape Horn.

# The Northwestern City

musician in Golden Gate Park

*The Palace of Fine Arts
and the Presidio*

    The Palace of Fine Arts, showpiece of the 1915 Panama-Pacific Exposition, was designed by Bernard Maybeck to commemorate the four hundredth anniversary of Balboa's discovery of the Pacific Ocean and to celebrate the completion of the Panama Canal in 1914. The Palace is silhouetted against the sky and reflected in a lagoon at its base. I came upon it on a day of dense fog when it appeared as an apparition in the middle distance—a dream, a myth, a romantic link with times long past. Restored in 1967, it is all that is left of the original thirty-two

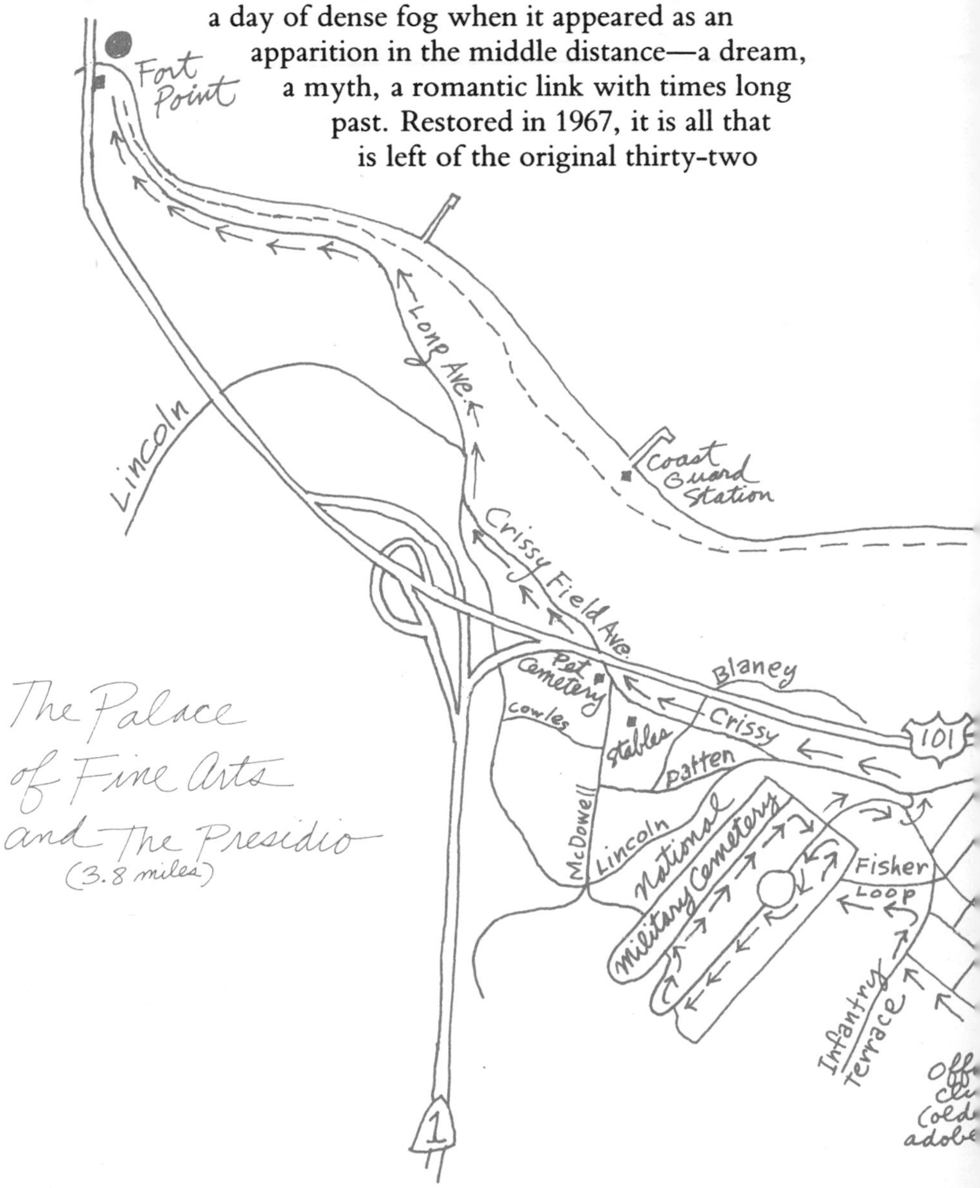

Fort Point

Lincoln

Lone Ave.

Coast Guard Station

Crissy Field Ave.

Pet Cemetery

Cowles

Blaney

Crissy

101

Stables

Patten

McDowell

Lincoln

National Military Cemetery

Fisher

Loop

Infantry Terrace

Off[...] Cold[...] adobe

*The Palace
of Fine Arts
and The Presidio*
*(3.8 miles)*

structures included in the Panama-Pacific Exposition. The remainder of the site is filled with Spanish Colonial Revival homes built during the twenties and thirties. The Palace of Fine Arts now serves a unique, practical purpose as the home of the very popular Exploratorium, a "hands-on" center where adults and children can touch, see, and learn about discoveries and innovations in the fields of science, art, and technology. The Palace of Fine Arts Theater is also here.

Lombard Gate, with its big guns on either side, is at the eastern margin of the historic Presidio of San Francisco. Juan Bautista de Anza claimed the area for the king of Spain when he and the first group of Spanish settlers arrived here in the spring of 1776. Upon Mexico's gain of independence in 1822, the Presidio was garrisoned by Mexicans, and on March 27, 1847, it was formally occupied by American troops. Originally sand hills and rocks, the 1,400 acres are now a registered National Historic Landmark.

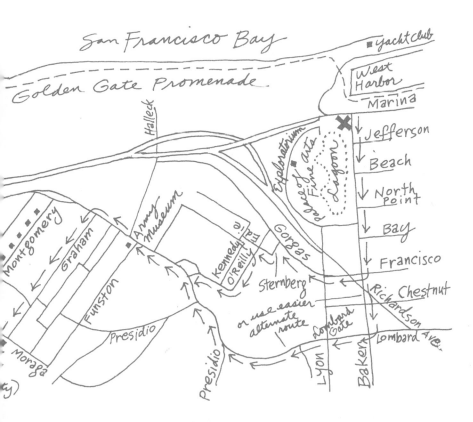

The Presidio Army Museum, located on Funston near Lincoln Boulevard, is housed in the Presidio's original 1863 hospital building. It was constructed of materials that came here by ship around Cape Horn. The museum, open Tuesday through Saturday, includes a wonderful array of pictures and displays ranging from old photographs of famous Indians to intricate dioramas. One diorama is of the Great Earthquake and Fire of 1906, but the most interesting, I think, is a diorama of the entire 1915 Panama-Pacific Exposition.

The Officer's Club is the site of San Francisco's oldest building, the 1792 headquarters of Lt. José Joaquin Moraga's Mexican army. Portions of the original walls remain.

The barracks, a fine row of brick buildings along Montgomery Street, feature strong, simple designs, each one relating to its neighbor. The barracks were constructed about a hundred years after the Presidio was established.

In the Presidio is a large National Military Cemetery. (The only other burial ground within the city limits, excluding the Pet Cemetery, is the small one at Mission Dolores.) I stopped here after Memorial Day, when each grave was decorated with a little American flag, and flags flanked both sides of the main avenues. A strong wind was blowing and the thousands of waving flags added color and motion to the rolling hills of stone markers.

There are more than 24,000 army personnel buried here, from Pvt. John Brown on July 23, 1852, of whom little is known other than that he was the first to be buried, to Gen. Frederick Funston, director of army relief during the 1906 disaster, to Gen. Hunter Liggett, commander of the First Army of the American Expeditionary Force in France in World War I. An interesting headstone is that of an Indian scout, dated 1873, which is simply engraved "Two Bits."

When you go past the old stables (on Patten) stop at the pine-shaded Pet Cemetery. You'll see markers here, among many, honoring such pets as Hula Girl ("We knew love, we had this little dog"), Skipper ("Best Damn Dog We Ever Had"), Patsy ("She loved fun"), Mr. Chipps, Pudge, and Bilbo Baggins, a white mouse.

The Bay and Palace of Fine Arts
from Baker and Vallejo Streets

# A Pleasant Route to the Legion of Honor

This journey fringes the wooded Presidio of San Francisco. Handsome, well-maintained, brown-shingled houses, some from the early 1900s, front along Pacific Avenue.

Number 3203 was built in 1902 as a wedding present from father to daughter. The wedding never took place, and architect Willis Polk was asked to design a larger dwelling. His solution was to raise the original house and add a story below. The 1902 houses at 3232 and 3234 Pacific were based on a Georgian design. Bruce Porter, a well-known artist-writer of his time, lived in one of them. Across the street, number 3233, with its distinctive Gothic windows and decorative gutter drain, was designed by Bernard Maybeck. On the north side of Pacific you'll note that each dwelling on the way down the hill is narrower than the one before so that the house at the bottom almost comes to a point.

The 1909 Roos House at 3500 Jackson is another Bernard Maybeck design, this one a modified half-timbered English Tudor style. It is striking, indeed. The large dwelling at 50 Laurel Street is a 1917 design by Bakewell and Brown, also the designers of the City Hall. Number 3340 Washington Street is an example of an architect's design appropriate for an eminent

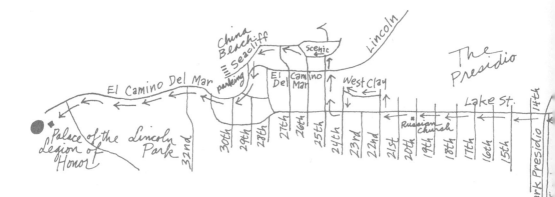

A Pleasant Route

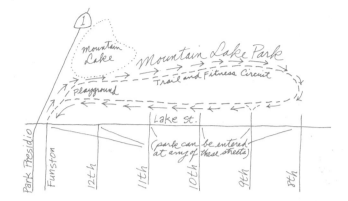

member of early San Francisco's French community. The brown-shingled Georgian Revival town house at 3362 Clay was designed by Willis Polk in 1896.

Charles Rollo Peters, well known for oil paintings of romantic subjects, designed the 1901 house at 3555 Clay. Noted landscape architect Thomas Church designed the grounds of the 1907 Greek Revival house at 3575 Clay. Three elegant houses circa 1900—numbers 3620, 3636, and 3652 —are also worth noting. The 1902 Koshland Mansion at 3800 Washington Street is, with its dramatic stairway, San Francisco's version of "Le Petit Trianon" in Versailles.

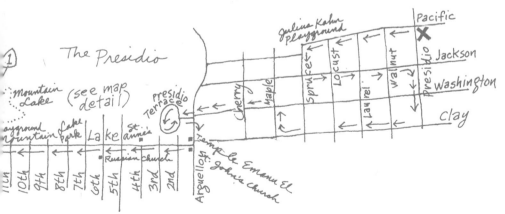

At Presidio Terrace a grouping of elegant houses stand as if in contemplation of one another. Number 30—with gargoyles yet!—looks as if it could have been the subject for a marvelous illustration I once saw in a children's storybook.

Temple Emanu-El's 150-foot-high domed interior is filled with inspirational light cast by the stained-glass designs of "fire and water" by San Francisco artist Mark Adams. In the vestibule, a Lucite work by the eminent sculptor Jacques Schnier is alive with inner light. The building itself is a Moorish Revival style, yet it has a California Mission feeling.

At Mountain Lake Park (see map detail) you'll find a delightful little playground, a lake, and a trail with fitness devices including everything from "Log-hopping" to "Achilles Stretch" for those interested in improving their health.

*The Golden Gate*

The 1903 house at 129 Twenty-fourth Avenue, almost obscured by the huge tree towering over it, is where the great photographer Ansel Adams once lived with his parents.

Strong classical motifs placed against plain surfaces typify architect Willis Polk's designs at numbers 9, 25, and 45 Scenic Way.

Visit tiny China Beach, described in the last chapter, on your way to the California Palace of the Legion of Honor. The Legion of Honor, dramatically located on a coastal hilltop with views of the Golden Gate Bridge, was modeled after the Palais de la Legion d'Honneur in Paris and erected in 1924. It houses changing art shows as well as a permanent collection of significant works, including the Achenbach Foundation for Graphic Arts collection of drawings and prints.

# The Eastern Edge of Golden Gate Park

Begin your walk at the corner of Fulton and Stanyan. You will soon sense the striking contrast here between the park and the commotion and concrete outside. (If you have driven to this point, you might find parking a problem. Try Conservatory Drive near the horseshoe pits, or Kennedy Drive. You can reverse the direction of the walk if parking is available at Mary B. Connolly Children's Playground.)

The horseshoe pits look professionally laid out. They are embellished at one end by a gigantic bas-relief of a yellow horse and, to the side, by another called "The Horseshoe Pitcher." Both were done in the 1930s by Horseshoe Club member "Vet" Anderson.

Cross Conservatory Drive for a walk through the fuchsia gardens. You might find them, as I did, in full, vigorous bloom. The branches of great redwoods, pines, and cypress trees give a cathedral-like effect overhead.

Park Headquarters is located at Stanyan and Kennedy in McLaren Lodge, the Richardsonian Romanesque stone house built in 1895 for Park Superintendent John McLaren. In front is San Francisco's official Christmas tree, a huge cypress planted in 1875.

Cross busy Kennedy Drive—carefully—for a view of a statue that McLaren might have approved of, since it is well hidden by greenery and its green-gray weathered surface makes it particularly unobtrusive. The grim figure is that of Henry W. Halleck, general in chief of the Union armies of the United States, 1862–1864. McLaren irreverently referred to statues as "stookies" and he didn't want them in the park. When they were placed there, over his objections, he planted around them to disguise their whereabouts. Since his death, however, a "stookie" of McLaren himself can be seen at John McLaren Rhododendron Dell.

Sculptor Douglas Tildon created the baseball player that stands in full view along the way to the tennis pavilions. Past the busy courts there is a vast lawn, with the 1885 Richardsonian Romanesque-style Children's House in view across the green.

When you come to the 1889 Alvord Lake Bridge you'll be seeing the first reinforced concrete structure of its kind built in the United States. An interesting feature to note as you walk through the tunnel under the bridge is the cast–in–place stalactites. Alvord Lake itself is charming with its green frog–on–a–rock bubbling fountain.

End your walk at the first public children's playground (1887) established in the United States. There is a lovely carousel here, built in North Tonawanda, New York, in 1912. It was first used in California at the 1939 Golden Gate International Exposition on Treasure Island in San Francisco Bay. To the sound of the old German calliope you can ride a colorful giraffe, or a lion, dragon, cat, reindeer, horse, stork, tiger, rooster, and more!

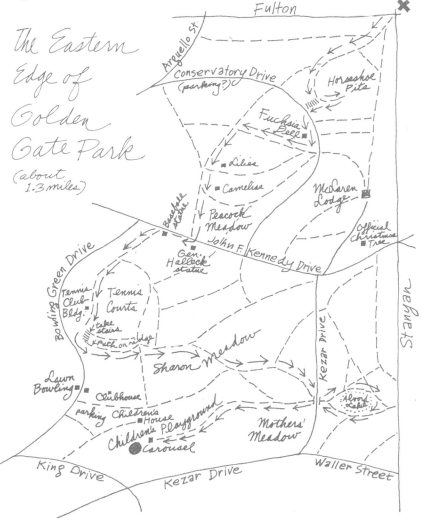

The Eastern Edge of Golden Gate Park (about 1.3 miles)

*The Conservatory in Golden Gate Park*

# Lily Pond to the Music Concourse

Golden Gate Park is San Francisco's true oasis, where thick forests muffle the hum of the busy city. As one local writer described it in 1924, "It stretches like a massive gold-green buckler enameled with lustrous gems." With the exception of fast walkers and joggers, everyone else in the park seems content to stroll leisurely or sink onto benches and lawns, disregarding the clamor outside its environs.

It was William Hammond Hall who helped win the argument as to where the park would be located. He surveyed it, made up a plan, and became its first supervisor in 1871. John McLaren became the park's fourth supervisor on July 29, 1890, and kept the job until his death at ninety-six in 1943. By that time he had planted more than one million trees.

The walk I have mapped for you is unusual in that it starts away from the attractions of the Music Concourse. This way you'll have a better chance to park if you come by car. Of course, you can join any of my walks and car trips at whatever point you find most convenient.

As my map shows, this walk begins just two-tenths of a mile from Kennedy Drive (Kennedy is closed to cars on Sundays between Kezar Drive and Transverse Drive, along Middle Drive East and on the right). The path is unmarked; but it is fairly obvious and just a short distance from Lily Pond.

Past Lily Pond turn right and walk through the exotic forest of tree ferns from Australia and New Zealand. The astonishing Victorian Conservatory, a replica of the one in Kew Gardens, London, can be seen in the distance. Continue walking and you'll come to the tunnel under Kennedy Drive. Go through the tunnel to reach the Conservatory and its fine collection of tropical plants. The Conservatory was originally designed for the private estate of James Lick near San Jose. Before it was installed, however, Lick died and the executors of his will sold the materials to a group of public-spirited San Francisco citizens who then had it erected in Golden Gate Park.

Other paths shown on my map will take you through John McLaren Rhododendron Dell and on to the Music Concourse where in mid-February the yearly pruning of elms and sycamores takes place. Surrounding the Music Concourse are six of the park's great attractions—the M. H. de Young Museum, Asian Art Museum, Japanese Tea Garden, California Academy of Sciences, Steinhart Aquarium, and Morrison Planetarium. This large invasion of Golden Gate Park's 1,017 acres by buildings was brought about when it was decided that the California Midwinter International Exposition of 1894 should be held here. A monument of Francis Scott Key, composer of our national anthem, had already been installed, having come from Italy in 1888. The Music Concourse dates from the Exposition as do the Japanese Tea Garden's Buddhist and Shinto shrines and half-moon Wishing Bridge. The Japanese-American Hagiwara family of gardeners cared for and nurtured the Tea Garden from 1894 to 1942. This devotion is memorialized in a unique plaque, designed by sculptor Ruth Asawa, on the left as you enter the garden. The "Wine Press" sculpture, opposite and east of the de Young Museum is also left over from the Exposition. The museum was completed shortly thereafter, in 1895.

Nearby all this is the Shakespeare Garden of flowers and plants where my family has had many a picnic. All the trees, shrubs, and flowers planted here are mentioned in the works of the great bard.

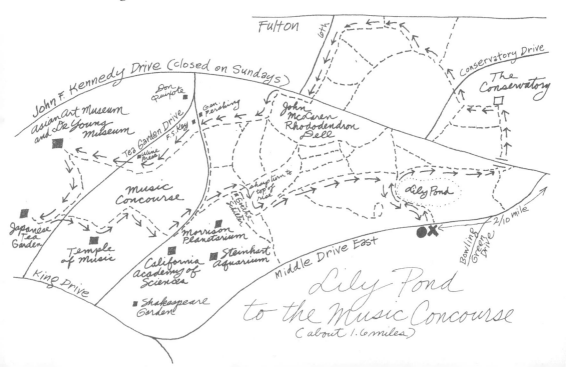

Lily Pond
to the Music Concourse
(about 1.6 miles)

*Pruning trees in the Music Concourse*

## Stow Lake, Strawberry Hill, and Strybing Arboretum

Golden Gate Park is not a great distance from any point in San Francisco. If you go by car you might find it convenient to park near the Rose Garden along Kennedy Drive, the main road through the park, and walk to Stow Lake. Here, you will see Huntington Falls and the Chinese Pavilion. The Falls, created by park designers, tumbles down a series of out-croppings of rocks. Stairs follow the Falls on both sides, af-fording a variety of views of the roaring cascade of water. The

Pavilion, a serene place to sit and unwind, was a gift from the city of Taipai on Formosa.

Cross the 1893 Rustic Bridge and ascend Strawberry Hill to enjoy an overlook of the Falls and a view east over the city. Originally, this hill was covered with scrub oaks and wild strawberry plants, most of them gone now.

Strybing Arboretum and Botanical Gardens are an inspiration to behold and a joy to explore. During your walk you might witness the glory of various plants in bloom. In early spring the Asian magnolia trees are in full flower. The Helen Crocker Russell Library here is available for research with a collection of 10,000 books on horticulture.

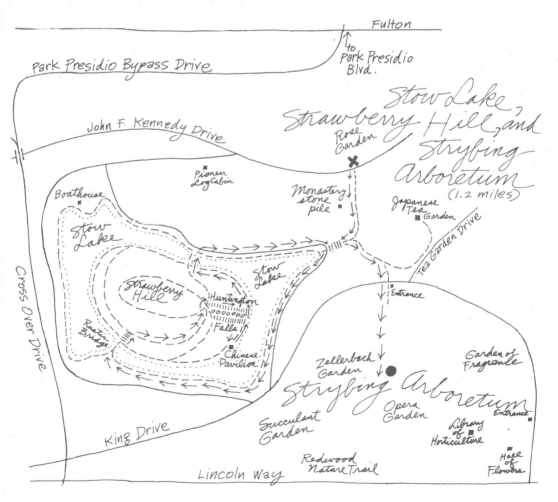

Strawberry Hill and Huntington Falls

# The Many Lakes of Golden Gate Park

On your lake tour first stop to see the source of Rainbow Falls, where water gushes from the rocks above as if by divine command. The concrete Prayer Book Cross, which stands above the Falls, dates from 1894 and was modeled after an ancient Celtic cross. It was placed here by the citizens of San Francisco to commemorate the first use, by Sir Francis Drake's chaplain in 1579, of the *Book of Common Prayer* on the West Coast.

Lloyd Lake, the next stop, is famous for its "Portals of the Past," the nostalgic ruins of A. N. Towne's Nob Hill mansion, laid waste by the 1906 earthquake and fire. The lake was named in memory of Reuben Lloyd (1835–1909), pioneer lawyer and park commissioner.

Journey from here to Elk Glen Lake and Mallard Lake, and to pretty Metson Lake, bordered by giant cypresses. South and Middle lakes are idyllic ponds with ducks and geese paddling about. People like to stand along the grassy shorelines and feed bits of bread to the friendly birds.

Chain of Lakes (North, Middle, and South) and Elk Glen Lake are all natural lakes that predate the creation of the park in 1870. Angler's Lodge and the fly-casting pool are worth

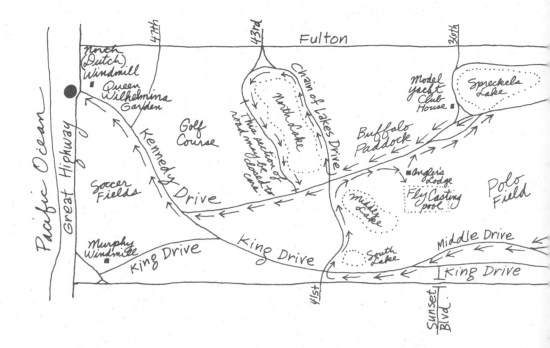

investigating. Buffalo are paddocked
along Kennedy Drive, and beyond there
is the unusual, man-made Spreckels
Lake. It is always full to capacity, good
for launching toy sailboats and radio-
controlled craft on extensive cruises.
I met an elderly gentleman who commanded a tug and barge from a comfortable
captain's chair. He said he could send
the craft anywhere he wanted to on the
lake right from where he sat.

After visiting North Lake, proceed
to the North, or Dutch, Windmill. In
1902 it could pump 30,000 gallons of
well water an hour as far as two miles
distant to water the park. The delightful
Queen Wilhelmina Garden is here between
the huge Dutch Windmill and windswept
cypresses. Murphy Windmill, at the
southwest corner of Golden Gate Park,
was the largest in the world when it
was completed in 1905.

Portals of the Past
at Lloyd Lake

The Many Lakes of Golden Gate Park
(4.9 miles)

# The Cliff House and Coastal Trail to Fort Point

The original Cliff House, built in 1863, was the victim of a strange accident. In 1887, an abandoned schooner carrying 80,000 pounds of dynamite pounded on the rocks below the Cliff House until its cargo exploded, damaging the building's foundations. Rebuilt, it burned down in 1894. Adolf Sutro, onetime owner of Cliff House and mayor of San Francisco, who had since purchased much land here, then rebuilt the Cliff House as an extravagant Victorian masterpiece. It burned in 1907. The fourth version of the Cliff House still stands, undistinguished as to architecture, but with a striking location above the crashing sea.

In our younger years, my wife and I would on occasion come to this Cliff House to enjoy sumptuous breakfasts. We would come during the week when it was less crowded and sit at a window with a view to the sea. Below, we could see the seals basking on the rocks.

Sutro built his own home above the Cliff House on land now known as "Sutro Heights," but then called "Chambers's Potato Patch." A Mr. Chambers had lived here and farmed potatoes that were choice and in great demand, but it was a long trip by mule to market them in downtown San Francisco and I imagine he was happy to retire.

In Sutro's day there were, besides the house, a conservatory, a maze of green hedges, a bathhouse, a swimming pool, statuary, trees, and flowers. The grounds were open to the public with a small charge only for swimming and "amusements." The Potato Patch and Sutro home, pool, and amusements are long gone, but the park remains open to the public. A few broken statues and many of the old trees are all that are left.

Across the way are the crumbling remains of Sutro's Tropic Baths, the end of Sutro's vision of an aquatic pleasure dome for the average man. The baths had opened in 1896 and featured six saltwater swimming tanks and one freshwater plunge, all of different sizes and temperatures. These were equipped with nine springboards, seven toboggan slides, three trapezes, one high diving board, and thirty swinging rings. I can remember the joy of being there myself as a young boy,

The Cliff House
and Coastal
Trail to Fort
Point
(about 3.8 miles)
(about 1 mile to
Legion of Honor)

Golden Gate Bridge

101

Fort Point

Lincoln

Kobbe Ave.
Memorial
of World
War II

Coastal Trail

Baker Beach

Golden Gate National Recreation Area

Bowley Rd.
Gibson

Lincoln

China Beach

25th

Mile Rock

Pacific Ocean

Land's End

Coastal Trail

El Camino Del Mar

Palace of the Legion of Honor

U.S.S. San Francisco Monument

Veteran's Hospital

Seal Rock Drive

Clement

Merrie

Point Lobos

Sutro Baths ruins

Sutro Heights Park

Geary

Cliff House

Seal Rocks

48th

Great Highway

Balboa

73

trying first this pool, then that. What a magnificent place it was! It closed in 1960 after serving for a period as an ice-skating rink and, finally, burned down in 1966. Large photographs of Sutro Heights, the Baths, and the Cliff House in their glory can be seen two flights down at the Visitor Center located at the north end of the Cliff House.

A Coastal Trail continues here along the cliffs to China Beach. A higher trail, if you choose a shorter walk, goes to the California Palace of the Legion of Honor. On a clear day the Marin Headlands, Farallone Islands, and Point Reyes are visible. The trail is a combination of paths, old military roadways, beaches, sidewalks, and even the roadbed for an 1888 steam railroad.

China Beach got its name from the Chinese fishermen that once camped here in the Gold Rush days. It is one of the

*The Pacific Ocean, Seal Rocks, and Cliff House*

few San Francisco beaches considered safe for swimming. (On some maps it is shown as Phelan Beach.)

Baker Beach, farther along the Trail, is not considered safe for swimming. It is, nevertheless, a popular beach and the surf fishing is sometimes good. Battery Chamberlain is also a part of Baker Beach, a massive defense installation once considered essential for San Francisco's protection.

If you continue to hike the Coastal Trail there are rewarding views of the ocean, the cliffs, and the Golden Gate. The Golden Gate itself narrows to less than a mile wide, and in 1542 explorer Juan Rodríguez Cabrillo sailed up the coast without seeing it. It was a Spaniard, Sgt. José Ortega, a member of the Gaspar de Portolá expedition in 1769, who first saw San Francisco Bay from land. In 1775 the ship *San Carlos,* commanded by Juan Manuel de Ayala, was first to enter the Bay.

Today the Golden Gate is spanned by the great bridge designed by Joseph Strauss, Clifford Paine, and Irving Morrow. It was Morrow's idea to paint the bridge red. He claimed the color would be a good foil for the browns and greens of the far hills and the most visible in the dense fogs that roll through the narrow strait, sometimes so low-lying and thick that only a ship's mast can be seen as the vessel sails out to sea under the bridge.

Pedestrians are allowed to walk over the bridge and back. The surrounding views are extraordinary.

The Coastal Trail will take you under the bridge and down to old Fort Point. To preserve and protect the Point, the Golden Gate Bridge engineers designed a special arch that would clear it. The fort itself, completed in 1861, and one of San Francisco's most unique buildings, was never called upon to defend San Francisco Bay. Restoration, begun in 1970, is still in progress, but the building is open to the public as a wonderful museum staffed by attendants in Civil War costume to add to the flavor of its past.

Out on the Bay along the eastern wall of the Point, skillful surfers can often be seen enjoying their challenging sport. It looks so dangerous!

*The Coastal Trail and Golden Gate Bridge*

# The Southwestern City

joggers through the tall trees of Sigmund Stern Grove

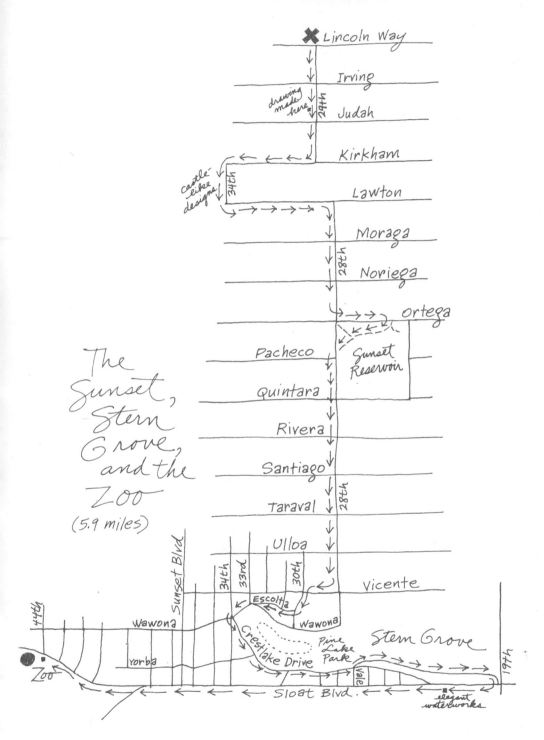

Lincoln Way

Irving

drawing made here

29th

Judah

Kirkham

castle like designs

34th

Lawton

Moraga

28th

Noriega

Ortega

Pacheco

Sunset Reservoir

Quintara

Rivera

Santiago

28th

Taraval

Ulloa

Vicente

The Sunset, Stern Grove, and the Zoo

(5.9 miles)

Sunset Blvd

34th

33rd

30th

Escolta

Wawona

Wawona

Stern Grove

44th

Crestlake Drive

Pine Lake Park

19th

Yorba

Zoo

Vale

Sloat Blvd.

elegant waterworks

# The Sunset, Stern Grove, and the Zoo

The houses of the inner Sunset District embrace one another in long rows. There is a pleasant rhythm and symmetry working here as row after row "march" down to the ocean front. Many of the dwellings seem to have expressions, from quizzical, placid, and languid to staunch, unconcerned, and jaunty—and more. The houses on Thirty-fourth Avenue resemble charming, family-size castles. At Twenty-eighth and Ortega, a reservoir placed high above is camouflaged by attractive landscaping. A pleasant walkway offers a panoramic view of the ocean, the Golden Gate, and north along the Marin coast. The faraway golden towers of the Russian church, Cathedral of the Holy Virgin, on Geary Street can also be seen. They gleam when the sun shines.

A path at Wawona and Thirty-fourth leads down into Pine Lake Park, then, at Vale Avenue and Crestlake Drive, continues down into Stern Grove, where tree ferns and redwoods grow and eucalyptus trees stretch to tremendous heights. The old Trocadero Inn, a resort in the 1890s, is still here. It was restored in 1930 under the direction of Bernard Maybeck, it is said. Free summer concerts in the Grove are very popular with San Franciscans.

The San Francisco Zoo has a new primate center and both visitors and animals are a joy to watch. I was particularly delighted by the antics of big-eyed douroucouli from South America that leaped and played in the almost-darkness of the Kresge Nocturnal Gallery.

*Houses along 29th Avenue in the Sunset District*

*From the Zoo to Ingleside, Saint Francis Wood, and Mount Davidson*

When you leave the zoo, continue on to Old Fort Funston, where a hike among dunes and dune plants will give you a real feeling for San Francisco's original terrain. Also, there is a spot here from which you can view hang gliders pitching themselves off high coastal cliffs, swooping and soaring like eagles. It's a fascinating spectacle when the wind is right.

Students from the University of San Francisco scull on the waters of Lake Merced, San Francisco's largest inland body of water. Off Lake Merced Boulevard, you can travel through Parkmerced District and the University's residential area to the Ingleside District. There, in Entrada Court, you will find the world's second largest sundial, or so boasted a local resident I spoke to. The tract builder's inspiration of 1913 is still telling time with accuracy, for at noon on the day I made my drawing the shadow was right there on XII. What a trusty design (barring foggy days)!

*The Sundial of Entrada Court*

On leaving Entrada Court, travel the delightful streets of Saint Francis Wood. In 1912 noted landscape architects Frederick Law Olmstead and John Galen Howard planned this development. The terrace and fountains on Saint Francis Boulevard were installed in 1913.

At Mount Davidson Park are at least three trails to the summit. You will enjoy the heady odor of eucalyptus as you hike to the crest where a concrete cross towers over the city. Early morning services are held here each Easter. San Francisco, the city of an infinite number of fine viewpoints, is seen from here at its highest elevation—nearly 1,000 feet.

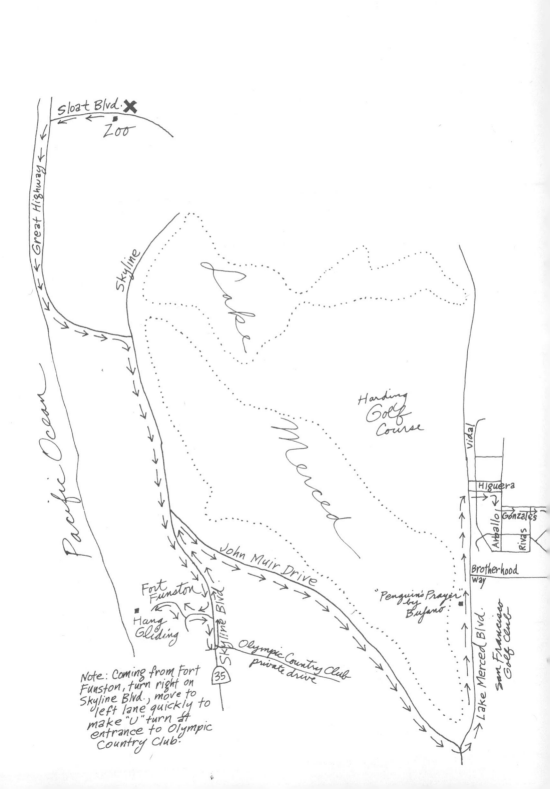

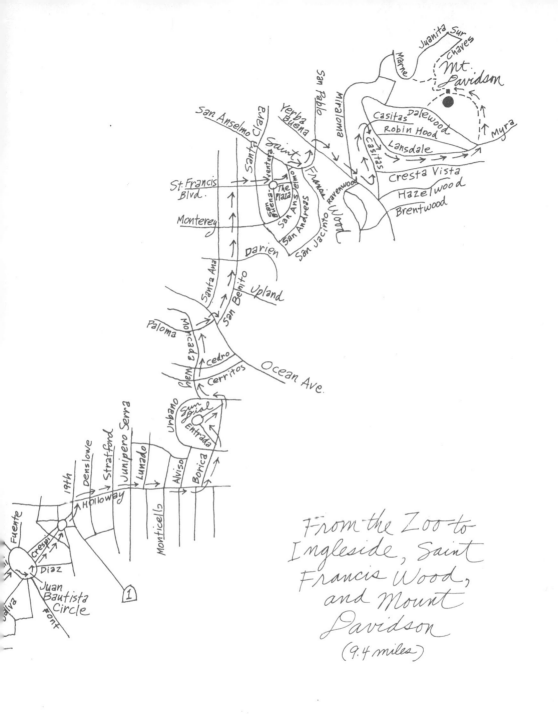

From the Zoo to Ingleside, Saint Francis Wood, and Mount Davidson

(9.4 miles)

Bell Mansion

# Exploring Glen Park District

Glen Canyon Park is tucked away in its own deep little valley between O'Shaughnessy Boulevard, Elk Street, and Diamond Heights Boulevard. On the slopes of Glen Canyon Park are interesting wooded streets and quaint houses. Number 301 Surrey hides behind a curtain of small trees, and the facade of 257 Surrey is adorned with two permanent wreaths with bows tied at the bottom. Perched high above the street at 190–198 Laidley is a large 1872 Victorian called Bell Mansion. It has a mansard roof and a grand stairway in front. From 1900 to 1916 it was the home of Teresa Bell, an associate of the well-known mulatto madam, "Mammy" Pleasant.

Number 153 Laidley has lovely carved ornamentation, while 123 is a very original design indeed with its big half-moon window, squared-off facade, and porch railings askew. Also high above Laidley, 118–120 is interesting for its massive glass walls and bold ornate railings. Number 11 Harper Street sits uniquely sideways to the street. At a little stone-and-brick house at the beginning of Sussex Street (number 15), I found a charming scottie dog gateway to draw.

Scottie Gate on Sussex Street

89

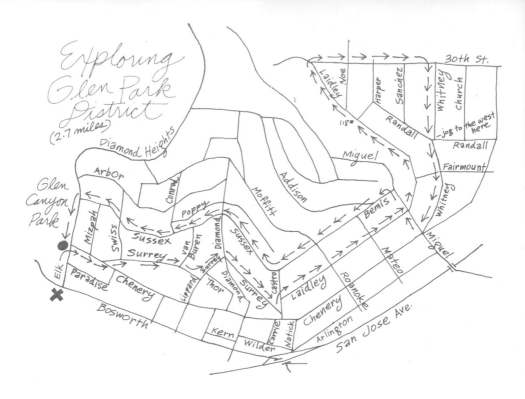

# A Trip through Forest Hills

I once lived near Ninth Avenue and Moraga Street and admired the homes above in Forest Hills. I still enjoy the trip up Eighth Avenue to enter Forest Hills and I'm sure you'll find it worthwhile, too. Some trees have grown to colossal size, including a holly tree on the west side of Eighth between Lawton and Moraga, and so have giant palms and cactus at Castenada and Alton avenues. Number one Marcella at Magellan is a 1921 pointed-roof "Mother Goose" design with a birdhouse nestled in the point. The grand stairway at Magellan and Pacheco is shown in my illustration.

Forest Hills was designed in 1915, no doubt by a land-scaper of great sensibility. The streets are aligned with the contours of the land, and the houses stand free of one another with ample landscaping between. Numbers 270 Castenada (1916) and 51 Sotelo (1915) are more Bernard Maybeck designs, as is 381 Magellan, which was built on weekends by members of the Forest Hills Association. Another "Mother Goose" design can be seen at 50 Montalvo Avenue.

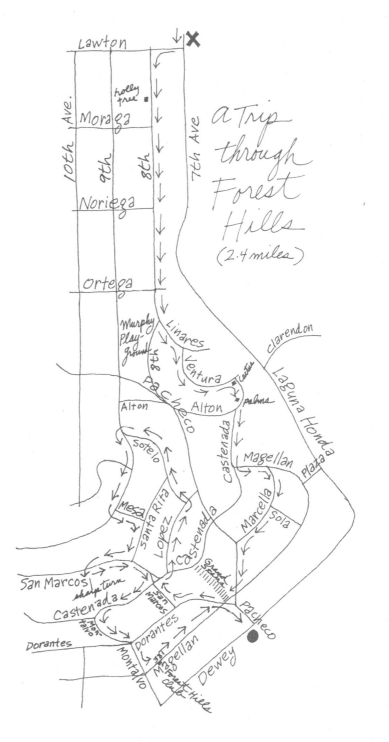

A Trip
through
Forest
Hills
(2.4 miles)

The Grand
Forest Hills Stairway

# High Roads and Cliff Dwellings

Hilltop parks, high-walled streets, and steep stairways are featured in these upper levels of the city.

Drive along Lawton Street and turn left on Lomita to view the crest of Grand View Park, then proceed along Aloha to Fifteenth Avenue, Fourteenth Avenue, Quintara, and Cragmont to Sunset Heights Park. A pine forest encircles the park, and ancient cypress trees of immense proportions flank the west side of the slope.

Walking is part of this tour, so park near Aerial Way and Pacheco Street. By following my map, you'll flex leg muscles on streets and stairways that lead to the "grand view" of Grand View Park. The stairs end in sand, driven to this high point from the ocean's shore by strong, ever-insistent winds. This is one mighty sand dune! The view from here is all-encompassing, perhaps the greatest view from any point within the city. (But one says that from most hilltops in San Francisco.) The eye sweeps across San Francisco from Twin Peaks to Mount Sutro, from the downtown skyline to Berkeley and the Bay, Angel Island, the Golden Gate, the coast north, Seal Rocks, Ocean Beach, and the coast south.

Later you can return to your car via Fourteenth Avenue, Ortega Street, Cascade Walk, and Pacheco Street to Aerial Way.

If you really want to develop your leg muscles, you can begin this tour by parking at Sixteenth Avenue and Kirkham Street where the Mount Everest of stair climbs goes to the top of Grand View. On the way up, make some rest stops and enjoy the ever-changing views.

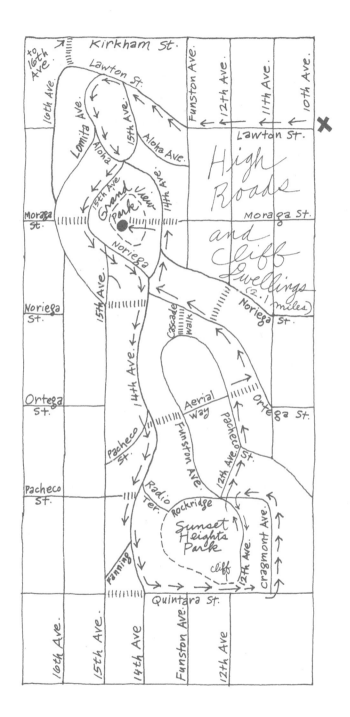

The Big Sand Dune, Grand View Park

## Twin Peaks, Corona Heights, Buena Vista, and the Haight

Twin Peaks offers a magnificent city view. The nineteenth-century historian Hubert Howe Bancroft called the view "the throne room of an imperial city." From here San Francisco resembles pieces of a puzzle, but all in place. Houses and buildings extend over the hills uninterrupted except for here and there where the hills break through. The generally "white" city spreads out below to the Bay where Alcatraz rides like a mighty battleship. Two bridges, one red, one silver, span the Golden Gate and Bay. Hills and mountains overlap on the horizon and on into infinity. In early spring, poppies, lupine, wood sorrel, and buttercups bloom on Twin Peaks and the hills are green.

If you wend your way down and then up again to Corona Heights, you'll come to the Josephine Randall Junior Museum, which houses a variety of creatures, from Costa Rican wood roaches to tropical American boa constrictors. Visitors are sometimes allowed to hold the massive snakes. Here I sketched Jocko, for thirty years the resident horned owl.

*Jocko*

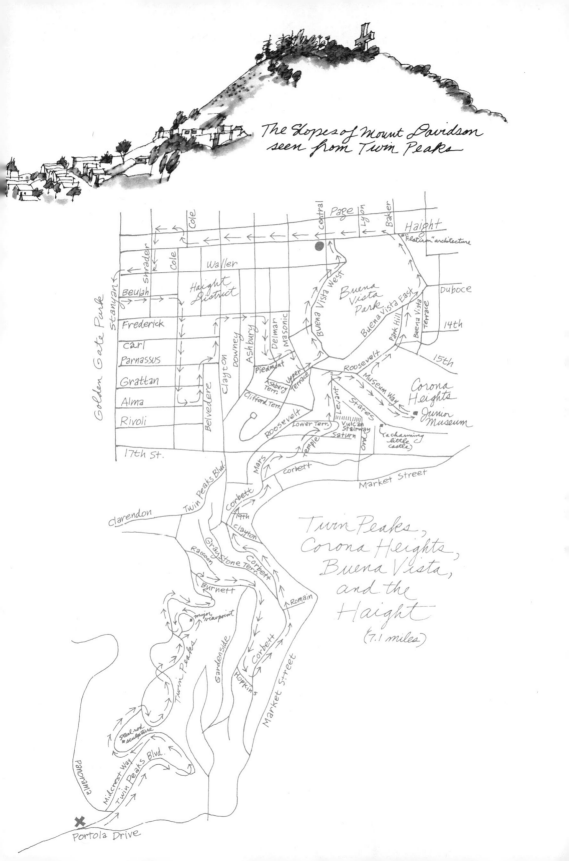

The Slopes of Mount Davidson
seen from Twin Peaks

Cole
Cole
Central
Page
Lyon
Baker
Haight
"Flatiron" architecture

Shrader
Waller
Stanyan

Beulah
Haight District
Buena Vista West
Buena Vista Park
Buena Vista East
Duboce

Frederick
Carl
Parnassus
Downey
Ashbury
Delmar
Masonic
Buena Vista West
Buena Vista Terrace
14th

Grattan
Clayton
Piedmont
Roosevelt
Park Hill
15th

Golden Gate Park
Belvedere
Ashbury Terr.
Upper Terrace
Museum Way
Corona Heights

Alma
Clifford Terr.
Levant
States
Junior Museum

Rivoli
Roosevelt
Lower Terr.
Saturn
Vulcan Stairway
Ord
"a charming little castle"

17th St.
Temple
Corbett
Market Street

Twin Peaks Blvd.
Mars
Corbett

Clarendon
Corbett
19th
Clayton

Twin Peaks, Corona Heights, Buena Vista, and the Haight

(7.1 miles)

Raccoon
Graystone Terr.
Corbett

Burnett
Romain

major viewpoint
Gardenside
Corbett

Twin Peaks
Hopkins
Market Street

steel rod sculpture

Panorama
Midcrest Way
Twin Peaks Blvd.

✕ Portola Drive

Corona Heights was
quarried at one time and its
shape somewhat mangled. Rem-
nants of an old iron kiln can be seen
on the hike to the top of the hill. On my climb, I stopped
to watch oak trees, coyote brush, and poppies being planted
on the slopes by the Junior Museum staff.

Buena Vista Park and its many walkways are worth
hiking. I drew ancient cypresses here where a wooden
stairway invited me to further exploration.

The individually designed and painted houses of the
Haight-Ashbury District create eye-catching combina-
tions of colors and patterns. Number 1–7 Buena Vista East
is a "flatiron" building, quite narrow at its western end.
Novelist Kathleen Norris once lived in the 1896 house at

*Stairway in*
*Buena Vista Park*

1901 Page Street, and the 1896 firehouse at 1757 Waller is another vision of old San Francisco. Number 130 Delmar dates from 1890 and displays an imaginative use of the Stick-Eastlake Victorian design. The dairy farmhouse at 11 Piedmont has the look of an early New England structure. Built in 1860, it was moved here in 1888 when its previous location was becoming overrun by houses of newer design. Number 1526 Masonic, designed by Bernard Maybeck in 1909, has an arrowhead design on one shutter, emblematic of the owner's passion for Indian lore. Note the imaginative wrought-iron gate at 731 Buena Vista West. The top floor of 737 Buena Vista West once held studios for writers Ambrose Bierce and Jack London.

St. Ignatius Church and the Marin Hills
from Buena Vista Park

# The South and Eastern City

320

*Neighborhood businesses*

# To Mission Dolores and the Mission

Before this area was crowded with apartments, the charming 1875 house at 3224 Market Street stood alone—the only house on the block. Below Market, tree-lined Caselli Street has many houses on its south side whose occupants must mount three flights of stairs to reach their front doors. Where Caselli meets Douglass (number 250) you'll see an enormous baroque Queen Anne Victorian home with "candlesnuffer" domes. The house was so costly to build

($100,000 in 1892) that neighbors named it "Nobby Clarke's Folly" after its wealthy owner, a local character.

There is a smooth concrete slide for young folks at diminutive Seward Street Park. A row of Stick–Eastlake Victorian houses runs from 717 to 733 Castro. There are many well-maintained historic houses along Liberty Street and a row of eleven nicely restored homes along Twenty-second Street (shown in my illustration).

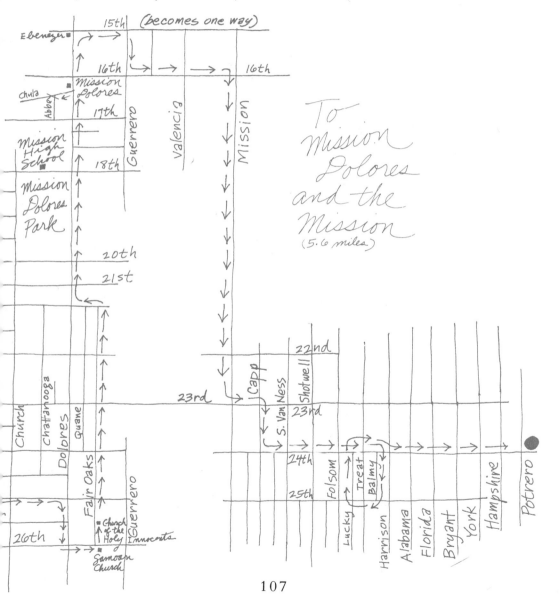

The First Samoan Congregational Church is at the foot of Fair Oaks Street. Numbers 464 and 435 are good examples of Stick-Italianate Victorian homes. In between the houses here you'll find the little Church of the Holy Innocents, with a red door. The 1895 house at 394 Fair Oaks is an interesting

*Homes along 22nd Street*

combination of late Eastlake, Queen Anne, and "period" architecture, while number 387, built in 1897, is unusual with its facade of scrolls and garlands.

Take a walk in Mission Dolores Park for its panoramic views and green expanses. Mission High School has a handsome Spanish Colonial tower that sparkles on a sunny day.

Mission Dolores was completed in 1791 and is the city's
most revered structure. Early San Franciscans buried within its
four-foot-thick walls include William Leidesdorff, black
pioneer businessman from the Virgin Islands; the Noe family,
important early residents of the city; Lt. José Joaquin Moraga,
leader of the group that established the Mission in 1776; and
the Very Reverend Richard Carroll, first pastor of Mission
Dolores after San Francisco became an archdiocese.

The former Notre Dame School, which was built in 1907, still stands across Dolores Street from the Mission. It has a mansard roof and an elegant stone fence with an iron gate.

Behind the Mission, 23 and 37 Abbey Street typify the flat-front Italianate design of the 1870s and 1880s.

At 214 and 220 Dolores Street, the Tanforan Cottages, where the prominent Toribio Tanforan family once lived, are very old, simple, one-story classical revival homes.

The 1904 church at Fifteenth Street and Dolores, which I attended in my younger years, was once the handsome, brown-shingled Ebenezer Lutheran Church; it has since been stuccoed. An Italianate house at 1876 Fifteenth Street is all that is left of an old Mission District tract.

You will find a Mexican-American atmosphere along colorful Mission Street, an avenue of tall palms. Wares from the markets spill out onto the sidewalks, and there are usually throngs of people busily shopping. Along Twenty-fourth Street, turn on to Balmy Street to see the brightly colored murals, depicting Mexican-Americans, and the amusing work of art strung out along a fence—a bas-relief clothesline with clothes attached. These are not permanent pieces, however, so you must appreciate them while you can.

Mission Dolores

## A Potrero Hill Trip

Along Kansas, from Division to Seventeenth Streets, attractively refurbished old warehouses serve as wholesale showrooms of merchandise for designers and decorators. Beyond "The Benches," at the end of Eighteenth Street, there is an overhanging pedestrian walkway. Cars and trucks pass underneath at dizzying speeds, creating a thrilling and terrifying effect on someone who doesn't regularly come this way. I dare you to try walking it!

McKinley Square Park offers its own panoramic landscape of San Francisco, a special Potrero Hill view. Vermont Street is only second in "wigglyness" to the more famous Lombard Street of Russian Hill. On Rhode Island Street, at 1101–1107, I stopped to draw these primitively designed walls with their abalone shell motifs. The white-painted plaster reminded me of faraway Greece.

The upper east side of Rhode Island Street has a number of houses with three-story flights of steps up to their front

Seashell Wall on
Rhode Island Street

doors, common with San Francisco hillside
architecture.

The Potrero Hill Neighborhood House
and Julian Theatre at 953 De Haro Street was
built in 1922. It was designed by architect Julia Morgan, known
for her work on Hearst Castle at San Simeon, California.

A 1915 firehouse stands at Wisconsin and Twenty-second
streets. Other notable historic houses to be seen along
Wisconsin Street include number 760, with its elaborate
wooden design over the porch, and numbers 731, 706, 627–
631, and 617. Corner house number 1788 on Twentieth Street
is the old Ramon family ranch house. The ranch originally
occupied much of this Potrero Hill District.

Along Connecticut there are seven Stick-design Victorian
homes in a cluster from 512 to 524. A flat-front Italianate
design at 555–557 and a Queen Anne–style home at 561 are
also worth noting.

Three Flights to the Front Door on Rhode Island Street

At 400 Pennsylvania is a well-kept Italianate house from the year 1870. A Capt. Charles Adams built the Italian villa home at 300 Pennsylvania in 1868. Across the street, number 301 dates from 1865.

Spirit Park, at Nineteenth and Minnesota, is a haven for a remarkable number of intriguing steel sculptures. The park is private—off-limits to the general public unless permission to use it is applied for at the neighboring building; however, the sculptures are clearly visible from a distance.

The diminutive shoreline of Agua Vista Park, distinguished by a large sign stating "Public Fishing Pier," is a good place to stop for lunch. Bring your own or enjoy the lively and popular restaurant next to the park, and view the boats and ships on the bay while munching.

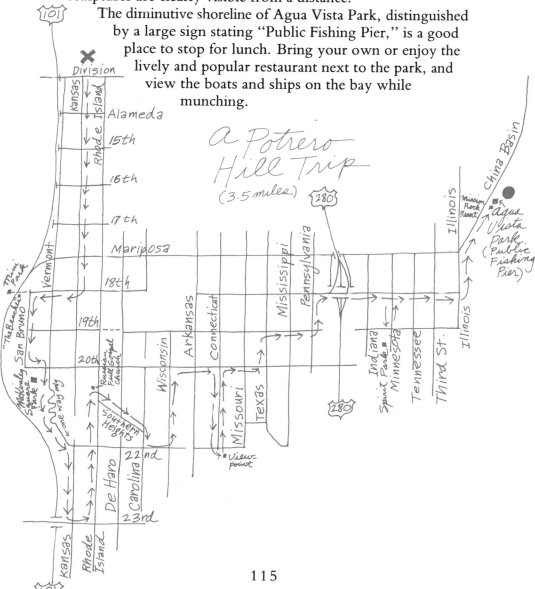

A Potrero Hill Trip
(3.5 miles)

115

# Agua Vista and along the Embarcadero

From Agua Vista Park you'll have views of big ships moored and in dry dock, freighters anchored out in the bay, others steaming by.

Leaving here you will see, along your way, piers in disrepair, factory areas, and views of San Francisco Bay. At China Basin, cross the huge, black contraption of a draw-bridge called Francis "Lefty" O'Doul Bridge after the former manager of the San Francisco Seals baseball team of yore.

Proceed on Third Street to South Park, a curious remnant of the once-fashionable Rincon Hill of the 1860s, the knoll from which the Bay Bridge springs. George Gordon, an English developer, laid out the park in 1854. I arrived there around noon and the place was peopled with a cross-cultural mix of San Franciscans enjoying their bag lunches.

You will pass the three-masted schooner *Dolphin P. Rempp,* seemingly permanently grounded at the Embarcadero (at Pier 42) as a restaurant.

As you approach the San Francisco–Oakland Bay Bridge, study the colossal silver cables rising from Rincon Hill and sweeping across the skyline.

A wonderful promenade stretches along the Bay on the way to the Ferry Building. A Ferry Plaza has been constructed stretching out over this part of the Bay where ferryboats once docked.

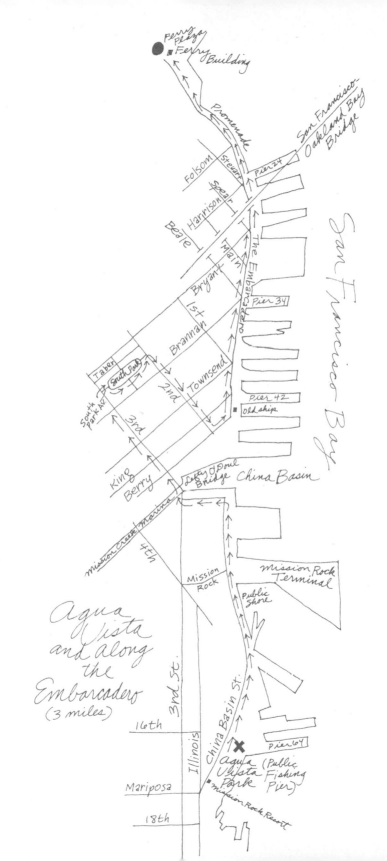

Ferry Plaza
Ferry Building

Promenade

San Francisco-Oakland Bay Bridge

Folsom
Stewart
Spear
Harrison
Beale
Main
Bryant
1st
Brannan
2nd
Townsend
Taber
South Park
South Park Ave.
3rd
King
Berry
4th
Mission Creek Marina
3rd St.
Illinois
China Basin St.
16th
Mariposa
18th

The Embarcadero

Pier 27
Pier 34
Pier 42
Old ship

San Francisco Bay

Lefty O'Doul Bridge
China Basin

Mission Rock
Mission Rock Terminal
Public Shore

Agua Vista and along the Embarcadero (3 miles)

✖
Pier 64
Agua Vista Park
Agua (Public Fishing Pier)
Mission Rock Resort

The Ferry Building, Promenade, and Ferry Plaza

# Candlestick Park and John McLaren Park to Crocker Amazon

The shape of the stadium at Candlestick Park is such that it looks like a colossal flying saucer come to rest. This is a windy spot but if you come between 8 A.M. and 11 A.M. it can be calm and sunny. I used to swim and sunbathe here with boyhood friends through summer vacations. Today the Candlestick Point State Recreation Area has facilities for fishing, swimming, sunbathing, and picnicking. Best make it a "breakfast picnic" because the wind usually comes up later in the day and the weather turns chilly. There are panoramic views here of land and bay, from the steeple of All Hallows Church to the Hunters Point docks, from the little town of Brisbane to the hills beyond.

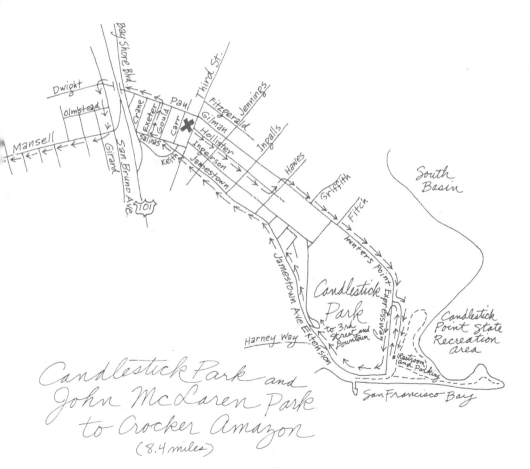

Candlestick Park and
John McLaren Park
to Crocker Amazon
(8.4 miles)

*View of the City from McLaren Park*

Near San Francisco's southern limits is John McLaren Park. Vast hills of eucalyptus, pine, and cypress groves, city views, and recreational facilities can be found here. I sketched the landscape shown when the sun was setting and the distant city was aglow with sharp, glancing light from the west. People, home from the day's work, were walking their dogs along the many paths. A brisk, chilly wind blew.

While I was in the area, I visited the Crocker Amazon neighborhood where I lived when I was a young schoolboy (I was surprised at how little my old district had changed in over fifty years). Back in those days, I liked to take a different route each day to Guadalupe Grammar School from my home on Morse Street. It was the beginning of my lifelong fascination with travel and the enjoyment of searching out interesting and unusual routes to somewhere—anywhere—in the world.

*Author's note:* There is a lift bridge over Islais Creek in a subtle but interesting streamlined Art Moderne architectural style. Out on Hunters Point at 881 Innes Avenue you'll see old stone buildings with terraced gardens, quite historic in appearance. This was once the 1870 Albion Brewery. The springs here are still in use, now by Mountain Spring Water Company.

The South San Francisco Opera House at Newcomb and Mendell had plenty of patrons in the olden days at this astonishing way-out-of-the-way location. It opened Christmas week, 1888, with a performance of "Little Puck." Evidence of the affluence of the area at that time is the magnificent wooden Gothic All Hallows Church (1886) at Newhall and Palou. Huge palm trees, planted during the same era, decorate the middle of Quesada Avenue nearby. At 1556 Revere an arresting, ornate house built in 1870 is still in good repair.

Haight Street Shop Window

## Some of San Francisco's Most Colorful Neighborhood Shopping Streets

BROADWAY—*Powell Street to Columbus Avenue*

CASTRO STREET—*Market Street to Nineteenth Street*

CHESTNUT STREET—*Fillmore Street to Sacramento Street*

CLEMENT STREET—*Arguello Boulevard to Funston Avenue*

COLUMBUS AVENUE—*Greenwich Street to Pacific Avenue*

EIGHTEENTH STREET—*Texas Street to Connecticut Street*

FILLMORE STREET—*Bush Street to Washington Street*

GRANT AVENUE—*Columbus Avenue to Filbert Street*

HAIGHT STREET—*Masonic Avenue to Shrader Street*

IRVING STREET—*Seventh Avenue to Tenth Avenue and Nineteenth Avenue to Twenty-seventh Avenue*

MISSION STREET—*Nineteenth Street to Twenty-fifth Street*

POLK STREET—*Bush Street to Jackson Street*

STOCKTON STREET—*Sacramento Street to Columbus Avenue*

TWENTY-FOURTH STREET—*Mission Street to York Street and Church Street to Castro Street*

UNION STREET—*Steiner Street to Gough Street*

WEST PORTAL AVENUE—*Ulloa to Fifteenth Avenue*

# Select Bibliography

Listed below are some of the many books I enjoyed in my research.

Baer, Morley; Pomada, Elizabeth; and Larsen, Michael. *Painted Ladies: San Francisco's Resplendent Victorians.* New York: Dutton, 1978.

Bakalinsky, Adah. *Stairway Walks in San Francisco.* San Francisco: Lexikos Publishing, 1984.

Clary, Raymond H. *The Making of Golden Gate Park: The Early Years, 1865–1906.* San Francisco: Don't Call It Frisco Press, 1985.

Cole, Tom. *A Short History of San Francisco.* San Francisco: Lexikos Publishing, 1981.

Doss, Margot P. *San Francisco At Your Feet: The Great Walks in a Walker's Town.* Rev. ed. New York: Grove Press, 1980.

Gebhard, David, et al. *A Guide to Architecture in San Francisco and Northern California.* Layton, Utah: Peregrine Smith, Inc., 1973.

Gilliam, Harold. *The San Francisco Experience.* New York: Doubleday, 1972.

Junior League of San Francisco. *Here Today: San Francisco's Architectural Heritage.* San Francisco: Chronicle Books, 1968.

Liberatore, Karen. *The Complete Guide to the Golden Gate National Recreation Area.* San Francisco: Chronicle Books, 1982.

Olwell, Carol, and Waldhorn, Judith. *A Gift to the Street.* New York: St. Martin's Press, 1982.

---

If you find anything in error, or if there is information that you feel should be included in the next edition, please write to Earl Thollander in care of Clarkson N. Potter, Inc., 225 Park Avenue South, New York, New York 10003.

# *Index*